Analyzing Performance Problems

or You Really Oughta Wanna

How to figure out why people aren't doing what they should be, and what to do about it

Third Edition

Robert F. Mager
Peter Pipe

CEP PRESS
A wholly owned subsidiary of
The Center for Effective Performance, Inc.

Atlanta, Georgia

D0089599

Books by Robert F. Mager

Preparing Instructional Objectives, *Third Edition**

Measuring Instructional Results, *Third Edition**

Analyzing Performance Problems, *Third Edition**
(with Peter Pipe)

Goal Analysis, *Third Edition**

How to Turn Learners On . . . without turning them off, *Third Edition**

Making Instruction Work, *Second Edition**

What Every Manager Should Know About Training

Life in The Pinball Machine
* Sold as a six-volume set (The Mager Six-Pack)

About CEP

CEP helps organizations profit from planned changes such as mergers, acquisitions, re-structuring, globalization and ERP implementations. Using Dr. Robert F. Mager's renowned research-based methodology, our consultants help clients avoid the workforce performance problems that are likely to prevent them from achieving the results they expect from implementing strategic change.

We have the strategies, training, tools and resources to make your workforce a true competitive advantage.

Workforce Performance...WE WROTE THE BOOK.

For more information, contact:
CEP
1100 Johnson Ferry Road, Suite 150
Atlanta, GA 30342
(770) 458-4080 or (800) 558-4237

ISBN 1-879-618-17-6 (PREVIOUSLY ISBN 1-56103-336-7)
ISBN 1-879-618-15-X (SIX VOLUME SET)
Library of Congress Catalog Card Number: 96-72446
Printed in the United States of America

05 04 03   10 9 8 7 6

Contents

Introduction
Considering the Whole

People do things for the strangest reasons. For equally strange reasons, they also don't do things. Looking at society as a whole, at other people both old and young, in the world of work and elsewhere, and noting their apparent shortcomings, we are tempted to conclude:

"They don't have the right attitude . . ."

"They don't understand. We've got to teach them to . . ."

"They're just not motivated . . ."

"We've told them and told them, and they still don't . . ."

"We've got a training problem. . ."

Each of those statements, and many more like them, express discontent with what someone is doing. Each comments on what is perceived to be a problem in need of a solution. And each, because of the way it's phrased, suggests something about what the solution should be.

It would be a mistake, though, to take these comments at face value and, in particular, to think that a solution to the problem has been found. That's a rush to judgment, because people don't do what's expected of them for many reasons. Unless steps are taken to understand the problem before solutions are applied, substantial resources might be committed while at the same time leaving the problem unsolved.

If we label others as having *poor attitude* and *lack of motivation,* we are finger-pointing, naming a culprit and hinting at a solution instead of probing for the problem by asking, "Why is this so? What causes it?" Similarly, we jump the gun if we look at inadequate performance and declare, "We've got a training problem." Again, this confuses problem and solution. Training isn't a problem; it's just *one of the solutions* used to solve problems that arise *when people truly cannot do* what is expected of them.

The danger in leaping from apparent problem to apparent solution is that large amounts of time and money can be spent in throwing training at a problem that training cannot solve. Similarly, if you leap to a conclusion that someone's attitude needs to be "fixed" and that what it takes is "training" and perhaps a "good talking to," you can end up blue in the face and with nothing much changed. You need to dig a little deeper.

This is why a procedure like performance analysis is important to those who actually want to solve problems—rather than just talk about them.

Analyzing Performance Problems will show you how to seek out the real reasons why people don't perform the way they should, the true problems, and then help you match solutions to those problems. Mainly, we will discuss this in the context of the world of work, but, as you will see, these same ideas also apply anywhere that people are not doing what they should.

The procedure to be described is not unlike the quest for the villain in a mystery story, wherein the detective sorts through a collection of clues—some useful, some not—to discover the perpetrator of the dastardly deed. But rather than solving crimes, we'll work with problems in which what someone is expected to do is not the same as what that person is *actually* doing. Or, saying that another way, we'll be dealing with *performance discrepancies.*

Note that word *discrepancies.* We are being careful at this stage not to talk about performance *deficiencies.*

- If we say that someone's performance is *deficient,* it implies that there's something "wrong" with the individual whose performance doesn't match what we want. It also implies that something about the individual is what must be changed.
- On the other hand, when we talk of a *discrepancy,* we are simply recognizing that a difference exists between the performance we have and the performance we want; the two are simply not in balance. And if we could weigh them on a scale, we could bring them into balance by either subtracting weight from one side of the scale or by adding to the other, thereby increasing our options for solutions.

That last point about increasing options is important because (as we'll try to show you):

- People don't perform as desired for many reasons; for example,

    (a) they don't know what's expected;

    (b) they don't have the tools, space, authority;

    (c) they don't get feedback about performance quality;

    (d) they're punished when they do it right;

    (e) they're rewarded when they do it wrong;

    (f) they're ignored whether they do it right or wrong; and

    (g) they don't know how to do it.

- Often, what is identified as "the problem" isn't the problem at all.
- Proposing a solution before the problem is understood is

just shooting from the hip. (Taking action before the problem is understood can lead to unnecessary waste of time and effort, to unsolved problems, and to embarrassment.)
- The best solutions are not always found in the obvious places and often can be a blend of several solutions.

What's In It For Me?

Once you've learned to apply the performance analysis procedure you'll be able to solve the "mysteries" of performance problems in an orderly way. You'll be able to:

- Identify the causes of the problems,
- Decide which problems are worth solving,
- Describe solutions which will help you solve the problems, and
- Decide which solutions will be both practical and economically feasible.

By the time you are done, your new X-ray vision will help you see where expensive misfits exist between problems and solutions. You will see that some problems cost millions and others cost no more than the annoyance of the person perceiving the discrepancy as a "problem." You will find that sometimes providing information really is the answer; other times you will reach solutions that are too massive to put into practice and, maybe more often than you might think, you will find solutions that are easy to apply and cost only pennies or even nothing at all.

From Here to Mastery

To help develop your new X-ray vision, we'll describe and illustrate each of the steps of the procedure. So that you can see the sequence of steps and also keep track of where you are, we will center our discussion on a flow diagram (opposite). This is just a "map" that will remind you of where you are in the process. (Though it may look a bit formidable when you first

Performance Analysis Flow Diagram*

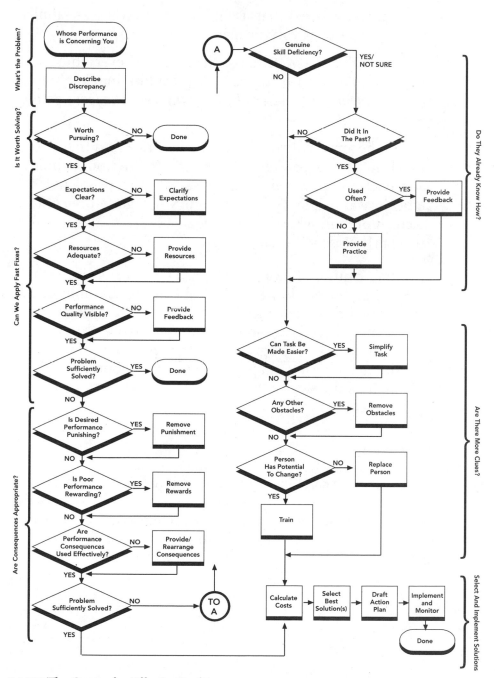

© 1997 The Center for Effective Performance

* An insert of the Performance Analysis Flowchart is found at the back of the book.

look at it, rest assured that it will quickly become as familiar and as easy to use as your favorite can opener.)

Caution: The diagram makes it look as if everything is neatly welded into place, each step leading inevitably to the next. *Don't be deceived by appearances. The formula is not that rigid.*

As you become skilled in using it, you may find that you can leap a step here and there. That's fine; our whole approach is designed to help solve your problem as quickly as possible. At first, though, you'll get more complete, more innovative, and more successful results if you stay fairly close to the steps as given.

Another caution: Beware the hazards of considering only one possible solution to any problem. That's only one stage better than viewing all performance discrepancies as problems of training—or attitude. To avoid this trap, you'll find the flow diagram, and the reminder questions at the end of each chapter, useful. Run your problem through all the steps before you decide that your analysis is complete.

What Now?

Because "you can't fix it if you can't recognize it," we'll begin by learning how to recognize and describe performance discrepancies. Before we do, however, we'd like to offer this happy thought: It will take a lot longer to describe and illustrate the performance analysis procedure than it will take you to apply it.

Part I
They're Not Doing What They Should Be Doing

We think we've got a training problem.

The procedure we are about to describe is one that shows you how to analyze the nature, the importance, the causes, and the solutions to things called performance discrepancies. Since you can't analyze one unless you know how to recognize one when you see one, we'll begin there.

1

What Is the Performance Discrepancy?

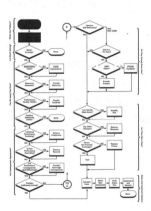

Someone has identified a "problem," and we are trying to determine the nature of the performance discrepancy.

A discrepancy is a *difference,* a mismatch, between *what is* and what *should* be. And our focus here is on *human* performance discrepancies, those differences between what *people* are actually doing (or not doing) and what they should be doing. As we proceed, we'll want to identify those discrepancies large enough to warrant action, collect clues that will lead us to one or more solutions, and select among those solutions those which are the most powerful, practical, and economical.

Performance discrepancies come in many shades. They may be tiny, mere pinpricks of irritation to someone, or they can be big enough to have significant impact on life and limb, or anywhere in between. They can exist in:

- *Personal interactions.* For example, the parent wants dirty clothes in the laundry hamper; the child leaves clothing in a pile on the floor.

- *Clashes with policy.* For example, the instructor wants assignments turned in on time; students offer excuses for bringing them in late.

- *Unacceptable work practices.* For example, workers are expected to follow safety rules; they find shortcuts around the rules.

All of those are performance discrepancies, differences between what someone is expected to do and is actually doing. All are what one might call "sins of omission," or perhaps "sins of substitution," costing somebody grief, discomfort, or money, or worse. Sometimes, discrepancies are caused by *too much* performance. You may have read about or even have encountered cases such as:

- The social worker too quick to destroy a family member through unwarranted accusations of child abuse.
- The editor who inserts his/her own thought here and there in an attempt to "improve" the manuscript.
- The truck driver who has too many accidents.

What Is the Performance Discrepancy?

Faced with problems like those above, the first thing to realize is that it's not useful to start out proposing an answer, as in "We've got to train/teach/motivate . . ." Nor is it helpful to lay blame, as in "These people are lazy/not motivated/careless . . ." Not one of these comments says anything about people performance; not one describes a performance that is or is not satisfactory. In each case, we need more information if something useful is to be done about the alleged "problem."

What you have to do is ferret out the discrepancies between what *is* (the actual performance) and what *ought to be* (the expected performance). Do that by asking questions about why someone believes there is a problem to be solved. For example:

Him: We've got a training problem.
You: Oh? Why do you say you have a training problem?
Him: Well, our welders are having too many accidents.
You: So what you want is for welders to have fewer accidents?
Him: Exactly.

With the discrepancy identified in terms of what people are or aren't doing, we can go on to find out how many accidents are "too many." Then, we can plan a course of action to reduce the discrepancy between what is and what is desired. And that may or may not call for training. Another example:

Her: These students just aren't motivated.
You: Ah. And what do they do that causes you to say that?
Her: For one thing, they don't come to school on time, and when they do show up, they rarely have what they need to get to work.
You: So what you would like to do is to increase the number of students who show up on time?
Her: Yes.
You: And you would like to increase the number who come prepared to work?
Her: Definitely.

What started out as a finger pointed at the students' motivation was clarified as a desire for them to start in timely fashion and ready to work. With the true discrepancy revealed, we can now explore why this state of affairs exists. Is it because the bus breaks down a lot, because the students can't tell time, or is it something else? Once the reason(s) for the tardiness are revealed, thoughts can be turned toward solutions. Similarly for the preparedness issue. Here is yet another example:

Mgr: I want you to teach these supervisors to be motivated.

You: Mmm. Just what is it they're doing that causes you to say that?

Mgr: Doing? It's what they're not doing that's the problem.

You: And what is that?

Mgr: Well, for one thing, they aren't managing. They spend too much time running the machines they used to run before they were promoted. They shouldn't be doing that. They should be managing.

You: So what you want is for them to spend less time operating machines?

Mgr: Absolutely! When they're operating, they're not managing.

The complaint was about motivation, but at least one of the performance discrepancies comes down to this:

Actual performance: Time spent operating machines

Desired performance: Little or no time operating machines

Whose Performance Are We Talking About?

You need to be specific about which person or persons are being discussed. Why? Because:

First, it helps ensure that you are dealing with a "people performance problem," not some other kind of problem.

If the problem has to do with something other than people's performance, it follows that an analysis of someone's performance is not likely to be useful.

Second, the answer to "Whose performance?" is likely to influence the selection of workable solutions. Take, for example, this statement:

"They need to be taught the right attitude about safety."

You don't have to be a rocket scientist to see that what will improve "safety" in the chemistry lab could well be different from what will improve safety in a foundry or an office. So you need to identify the target of the complaint, like this:

Mgr: They need to be taught to have the right attitude about safety.

You: Who does?

Mgr: Everybody working in the chem lab.

Now you're ready to start pinning down what the discrepancy is:

You: Why do you say they don't have the right attitude about safety?

Mgr: Because instead of washing their used beakers and putting them back where they belong, they just shout, "Prosit," and throw the beakers into the fireplace.

You can see that had we been dealing with bookkeepers or, say, musicians, not only would an apparent "attitude problem" take a different form, but the solutions would also be different, as in:

Mgr: They just don't have the right attitude about their jobs.

You: Who doesn't?

Mgr: Our sales people.

> *You:*   What makes you say they don't have the right
>   attitude?
> *Mgr:*   Because they refuse to use the sales aids that we
>   provide them.

In this instance, the quest will be to find out why the sales aids are not used, and then, if the aids really would be of value, to find ways of encouraging their use. But suppose the dialogue had played out this way:

> *Mgr:*   They just don't have the right attitude about
>   their jobs.
> *You:*   Who's "they"?
> *Mgr:*   Our legal staff.
> *You:*   Oh. Why do you say they don't have the right
>   attitude?
> *Mgr:*   All they want to do is litigate, no matter how
>   trivial the issue. It seems that the only tool in
>   their legal toolbox is litigation. They drive us
>   nuts.

Again, the initial complaint was about attitude. But because different people were involved, the discrepancies were different, which means that the solutions would be different. And even if the issue for the chem-lab folks, the accountants, the sales people, and the lawyers was safety, it would require different remedies, because "safety" means different things in different circumstances. So before you even ask about the discrepancy, find out whose performance is at issue.

Summing Up

A performance discrepancy is a difference between what is and what should be. These discrepancies can exist in personal interactions, clashes with policy, and unacceptable work practices. We must first identify the discrepancy before attempting a solution.

What to do

First, identify the person or persons whose performance is said to be lacking. Then describe the perceived performance discrepancy in terms of (a) what is actually happening, and (b) the desired performance.

How to do it

Ask these questions:

- Whose performance is at issue?

- Why do I (or someone else) think there's a problem?

- What is the actual performance at issue?

- What is the desired performance?

2

Is It Worth Pursuing?

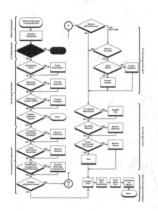

WHERE WE ARE

A performance discrepancy has been identified. Before we do anything else, we want to verify that it is worth continuing the analysis.

What Would Happen if We Let it Alone?

Different people see things in different ways. A situation causing some to just shrug their shoulders is seen by others as a Big Deal. The joke that tickles our funnybone may leave you wondering what the guffawing is all about. What to one is a spectacular sunset is to someone else just the end of another day. (Which is why the ancient Romans said, "One man's meat is another's poison.")

So when you first encounter a performance that seems to be pinching somebody, it's always appropriate to wonder if you are dealing with just a point of view that sees the "problem" as considerably larger than it actually is. The question to ask is: "What would happen if we let it alone?" If serious consequences would follow, then you have a discrepancy calling for further analysis. But if the only consequence of ignoring the "problem" is that it annoys the person describing it, then it probably isn't worth pursuing. Here's an example of just such a situation.

The Case of the Longhairs

Back in the days when the Baby Boomers were beginning to test their wings, the Beatles arrived in the USA to immediate success despite (Gasp!) long hair. Suddenly long hair was "in" for young males, not to mention some folks older than the Boomers. And equally suddenly parents and bosses began to sound off. "They oughta be ashamed of themselves," they said. "We've got to *teach* them not to look like bums." (Translation: They oughta wanna look like *me*.)

What was the discrepancy? About three inches of hair. Which led to this conversation with one manager:

"You are unhappy about the length of the new employees' hair?"

"Yes. It's disgraceful."

"Aside from your displeasure with long-haired males, what would be the consequence of ignoring it?"

"What do you mean?"

"What would happen if you let it alone?"

"Well, it probably wouldn't make much difference to business, but they ought to have more respect for the company. They ought not to want to look so sloppy."

In other words, the company would suffer no serious consequences. It just meant that some of the shorthairs would continue to be made uncomfortable (for awhile) by the presence of the longhairs. Hardly a reason for mounting a serious effort to eliminate the discrepancy, wouldn't you think? (Historical note: The world did not come to an end.)

But other companies had a different answer to the same question. To quote one machine-shop foreman: "Nobody in my shop wears long hair, or long *anything*. People with long hair, long ties, or loose clothing are a menace to themselves and maybe to others, because they can easily get caught in the rotating machinery."

Another manager said: "Most of our customers are shorthairs. If we send them a longhair sales rep, we just might put ourselves out of business."

So here, in two different settings, we have the same set of facts as before, but this time the response is not "Let it alone." In these settings, there is a consequence of some importance, and this time it looks as if the problem is worth pursuing.

Are Our Expectations Realistic?

Even if a problem cannot simply be dismissed (thereby saving yourself valuable time), one more step is needed before you commit to completing the entire analysis. The big question remains, "Should we ignore this discrepancy?" but this time the issue is, "Are our expectations realistic? What would happen if we succeeded?" Sometimes a little probing will show that it is less costly to ignore the discrepancy than to do something about it.

A Case of Success Would Kill Us

A sales manager with a force of more than a hundred people complained that they didn't heed his memo exhorting them to turn in a monthly article for the internal newsletter. The conversation went something like this:

Manager: "I've asked each person to send in a short article each month . . . less than a page . . . describing success stories or other interesting items. But only a few of them do it."

Analyst: "What happens as a result of your not getting articles from each person every month?"

Manager: "We don't hear about what they've been doing, and they don't get a chance to tell of their successes."

Analyst: "How much do you suppose that's costing in terms of dollars?"

Manager: "Dollars? That's hard to say. Nothing directly, of course, but we may be losing something in terms of motivation."

Analyst: "What would happen if everyone did as you asked?"

Manager: "What?"

Analyst: "What would happen if everyone sent in an article every month, just as you expect them to do?"

Manager: "Hmm. Then I'd have 112 articles for the monthly newsletter . . . ahh . . . gee . . . I see I'd have to hire another typist . . . and then I'd need another word processing terminal . . . uhh . . . we'd have to add a hundred more pages to our 12-page newsletter. That's a lot more than we can afford!"

Very quickly it became clear that the cost of eliminating the discrepancy would have been too heavy to bear. The solution? The sales manager readjusted his expectations, and the problem evaporated.

Summary So Far

When a performance discrepancy raises its head, it doesn't necessarily follow that you should rush into a full-blown search for solutions. Instead, follow these steps:

1. Ask: "What would happen if we ignored it?"

    If the answer is, "Nothing much," then the problem is trivial and can be set aside.

2. Ask: "What would happen if we succeeded?"

    If the problem cannot be easily set aside, then take a look at "the world as you would like it to be" and do a reality check.

    If it's plain that the cost of having the world as you would like it to be would be too high, that is, if the cost of "success" would be prohibitive, then stop.

On the other hand, if the problem's not trivial and the expectations are not unrealistic, then it's time to put on your Sherlock Holmes hat, get out your magnifying glass, and start digging (!). To solve the problem, you'll need to:

- find out more about the cost of the discrepancy,
- ferret out the causes and possible solutions, and then
- compare the cost of the problem against the cost of a potential "cure."

That will tell you whether it's time to act and, if so, what needs to be done.

How Big Is It?

Determining the "size" or "cost" of the discrepancy may not be a simple matter of adding up a few numbers. In some cases, direct costs are readily calculated—people are hurt, machinery is damaged, materials are wasted, or time is lost. Other times, the calculation is more obscure, as in lost sales, increased insurance premiums, or reduced production or quality. And sometimes, costs are intangible, such as loss of good will or morale or a tarnished company image. Yet all of these factors may be important in arriving at an estimate of discrepancy costs vital to deciding how much time and money a solution is worth.

But the moment you get away from direct costs and enter the realm of guessing about "what might happen if," move with care, because an attempt to assign costs to *potential* consequences can open a Pandora's box. In a paper mill, for example, workers were exhorted to replace the covers on fast-moving pulleys after working on them. But they weren't replacing them, and management said, "That's one of our problems. They should be putting the covers back on, but they *don't*. And that's dangerous. *Could* lead to serious accidents."

It *could*. But it never had. A check of the files showed that in the entire history of the company, not a single accident had been attributed to this "discrepancy." The maintenance people, apparently, were more careful than they were being given credit for (as is often the case). As a result, the *actual* "cost" of the discrepancy was zero.

But what about potential costs? Well, one might *speculate* that government safety inspectors, noting uncovered moving parts, might feel inclined to impose a penalty of a size clearly specified in such-and-such a regulation. Or that one or more employees might decide to sue because of an alleged exposure to potential harm. Or that an overzealous reporter might write a hand-wringing piece about the "dangers" of working for this company, thereby reducing the number of qualified job applicants and increasing the cost of insurance. Or . . . any of a thousand other "maybes."

The issue here is not whether hypothetical, as well as actual, costs should be considered when estimating the cost of a performance discrepancy, but whether such hypotheticals represent real and reasonably likely hazards. In the case in point, the coverless pulleys represent a known hazard; they are *known* to cause harm—even though they haven't yet done so in this company setting. Jaywalking also has been *known* to cause harm, so can be considered a likely hazard, even though only a hypothetical one to anyone not yet a casualty of this risky behavior.

Note that *potential* costs cannot be assigned only to performance discrepancies. One can catastrophize even about performance that is exactly correct, legal, moral, and ethical. The troubleshooter who performs according to all written policies and professional standards of conduct may still be fired, demoted, or even sued, over some alleged infraction. Physicians are routinely sued for malpractice, whether or not their performance has been exemplary. The hapless homeowner who damages an armed burglar in self-defense *could* find the cost of subsequent legal action running into the thousands of dollars. Driving legally along the highway *could* lead to loss of one or more lives in the case of an accident. (As our colleague Bonnie Abney points out, "You can be a terrific driver and still get pushed against a guard rail by a falling boulder.") And so on. Potential costs simply cannot be confined to performance discrepancies; *any* course of action could lead to any number of unexpected costs.

What to do? Add to the actual cost of the discrepancy the estimated cost of potential consequences, but only of those you can defend as being reasonably probable. Then, take remedial action to prevent the discrepancy from even happening, especially when such remedies are inexpensive and easy to apply. For example, in the case of the coverless pulleys, one might devise an inexpensive interlock that would prevent the machinery from turning on when the covers were not in place.

Possible Costs Arising from a Discrepancy

To get you thinking, here's a list of likely sources of costs. Usually, it makes sense to project such costs over a period of a year, so that you can report, "This discrepancy is costing us the whopping amount of _____ per year." If the project lasts less than a year, calculate the costs of the discrepancy over the lifetime of the project so that you can report, "This discrepancy will cost us _____ before this project is concluded."

Money. Is money lost directly (as when tellers or salesclerks give out more money in change than they should)? Are goods or materials lost (as through theft or accident)? Calculate the amount lost per year or the amount that would be lost per year if the discrepancy were allowed to persist.

Time. Do people waste time as a result of the discrepancy? Do they lose time because of materials shortages or lateness, because services are slow, or because defective work has to be redone? Is time lost because you or someone else worries about the discrepancy? If so, calculate the amount of time lost and its cost for a whole year.

Material Waste (Scrap). Is more scrap generated than is acceptable? How much more? What is the value of that scrap? What's the annual cost of having it hauled away or burned or remelted?

Equipment Damage. What is the cost of equipment damage resulting from the discrepancy? What's your estimate of the annual cost if the discrepancy continues?

Amount of Work Completed. Is there less production because of the discrepancy? What's the cost of the difference between the amount of completed work you are getting and the amount you should be getting?

Accuracy of Work Completed. Is the quality of the work suffering because of the discrepancy? How? And how much is it costing?

Insurance Premiums. Has the discrepancy led to increases in insurance premiums (as when drivers or others have too many accidents)? How much more per year are you paying?

Accidents. Does the discrepancy increase the frequency of accidents? Accidents can be costly, and most of the costs can be calculated. Add up the cost of workdays lost, hospital stays, damaged or destroyed equipment, and increased insurance premiums.

Even if the probability of an accident seems remote, the potential damage from an accident needs to be considered. When you can't accept the consequences of an accident, a potential cost needs to be assigned. Particularly when loss of life is more than a remote possibility, and particularly when someone may be legally held to blame, you are dealing with a potentially serious problem that cannot be dismissed as "not worth pursuing."

Lost Business. This one may be harder to quantify, but if someone says that a discrepancy is resulting in lost business, it is fair for you to ask "How much?" The answer may be only an approximation based on a review of sales records, but even an estimate provides better guidance than a mere guess.

Does the discrepancy require customers to spend more time waiting in line, filling out forms, waiting for the doctor, or returning items for repair? If so, there is a negative effect on the customer. Check to see whether the impact is resulting in lost business.

Duplicated Effort. Does it now take two people to do what one did before the discrepancy occurred? Are two departments now doing what only one did before? How much is that duplication costing?

Extra Supervision. Does the discrepancy mean that more supervision is needed than before? Do you need more guards, more security equipment, more monitoring time, or more monitoring equipment? Does someone spend more time overseeing? Does the supervisor end up doing the job himself/herself?

Other Costs. Will the discrepancy, or possibly the elimination of the discrepancy, lead to lawsuits? To sexual-harassment charges? To EEO complaints?

Multipliers Are Important

Earlier, we suggested that typically you should project the costs of a discrepancy for a year or some other significant period. In other words, don't look just at a single occurrence of the problem. Multiply it by the number of times it happens over a reasonable cycle. You need to determine: How many people are involved? How often? In how many places? You may find that what is judged to be a small problem can escalate enormously. Here's an example.

The Case of Late Displays

A young man working for one of Europe's biggest supermarket chains was learning to complete this kind of analysis. The only kind of problem he could think of, he said, was too trivial to bother with. As he explained, "Each week we send out displays for the weekly loss-leader items. And as often as not, a display sits in a market's warehouse and isn't set up until a couple of days into the week."

He estimated the amount of business lost through failure to "highlight the special" to be the equivalent of $100—too little, he thought, to make an examination worthwhile.

PP: Isn't there more than one loss-leader display sent out each week?

YM: Yes. And the people in the stores are sloppy about displaying them.

PP: Every week?

YM: Yes.

PP: How many stores are affected?

YM: Several hundred.

PP: So one hundred dollars lost per week per store, times several hundred stores . . .

YM: Wow! That could add up to as much as fifty thousand dollars a week!

You see the point. By the time we had multiplied all the various dimensions, this "trivial" problem was estimated to cost the equivalent of two million dollars a year!

But let's not get too pushy about the two million dollars. These were estimates, and although we tried to be conservative, perhaps the numbers were inflated. But even if the scale of the problem were only a tenth of what was estimated, that's still a lot of problem. If the true extent of the problem were only ten percent of the estimate, there's still a problem worth a substantial amount of a problem-solver's time.

When you have located and listed as many results or consequences of the performance discrepancy as you can think of, calculate, as best you can, the annual cost of each. When you add all costs together you will have quantified the total cost of the discrepancy and assessed its importance. Even though you may not be able to put a dollar amount on each of the costs, you will have a reasonably objective basis for deciding how much you can reasonably invest in a solution. In other words, you will be in a good position to compare the cost of potential solutions to the cost of the problem.

Summing Up

In deciding whether or not a solution to a performance discrepancy is worthwhile, we must determine what would happen if we let it alone and what could happen if we solved it. The costs and benefits of solving the discrepancy must be weighed against the costs and benefits of leaving it alone.

What to Do

Having identified a performance discrepancy that you or someone else feels is important to eliminate, check to see that the problem is truly a problem and not just an opinion, bias, or unrealistic expectation not worth pursuing. Reject if the problem is trivial.

If the problem is not plainly trivial, check that the expectations ("What we want to be happening") are reasonable, and reject the problem if they are not.

If the problem still survives this screening, find out what the discrepancy is costing. To estimate the size or value (and thus the importance) of the discrepancy:

- List all the consequences (outcomes) caused by the discrepancy.

- Calculate the cost of each outcome wherever possible.

- Total the costs.

How to Do It

Ask these questions:

- "What would happen if I let it alone?" If the answer is "Nothing much," the problem can be ignored. You're done.

- "Are our expectations reasonable?" If success in eliminating the discrepancy seems unlikely to achieve anything worthwhile, revise your expectations.

- "Does the discrepancy still survive?" If so:

  a. List all the consequences caused by the discrepancy.

  b. Calculate the cost of each outcome wherever possible. Use multipliers if appropriate (number of times the discrepancy is repeated over a period of, say, a year; number of sites; and so on).

  c. Total the costs.

  d. Do a final reality check by answering the question, "Is the cost of the discrepancy high enough that it seems worth pursuing a solution?"

Part II

Explore Fast Fixes

Are there obvious solutions that will help?

You intend to complete the entire analysis before selecting a course of action, of course; but before you do, you want to know whether you can apply some obvious "fast-fix" solutions that can make the performance discrepancy smaller or even go away.

3

Can We Apply Fast Fixes?

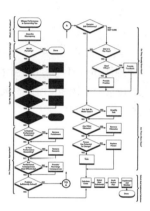

WHERE WE ARE

We have a performance discrepancy to eliminate, and the cost indicates that it's worth pursuing. Before going further with the analysis we want to see if we can end or reduce the discrepancy by a simple, easy-to-apply remedy.

Now that a performance discrepancy has been identified, and we have verified that the problem is big enough to warrant action, you may feel that it would make sense to move in with a complete analysis in the hunt for solutions. Not yet. Experience shows that many discrepancies are readily eliminated with little effort or expense. And even when you can't take care of the entire problem this way, you may solve enough of it to be hailed as a hero (after which you can belt out a lusty chorus of: *Put'cher finger in the dike, Mabel, before we spring another leak).*

Invisible Expectations

The first place to look for fast-fix possibilities is under a rock labeled "invisible expectations." When people don't know what they're expected to do or to accomplish, it is unlikely that their performance will meet expectations. You know you're in the presence of this category when you hear, "Nobody told me."

The Case of the Befuddled Draftees

Come with us to an aircraft builder's drafting department. Engineers were using the same symbols on drawings that they had used for their last employer. The situation looked like this:

Who?	Engineers
Actual Performance:	Using "wrong" notation on blueprints
Desired Performance:	Use notation prescribed by company

You ask a simple question ("Do they know what's expected of them?") and find that nobody has ever told these engineers what the desired notation was. They never were issued a copy of the notation policy, let alone a reminder sheet to hang over their desks. You might say to yourself, "Wait a minute. They're not doing what they're supposed to be doing—because nobody ever *told* them what they were supposed to be doing. We could solve this thing in a minute simply by letting them in on the secret." And you'd be right. All it took to put things right was to let them in on the secret of what was expected.

The clues that you may be dealing with invisible expectations sound like this:

"You never told me you wanted me to do it."

"You never said you wanted it done like *that.*"

"How was I supposed to know you wanted it today?"

"They may have changed it in the spec book, but nobody told *us* about the change."

The Case of the Secret Agenda

The secret agenda is too common in industry. It often shows up in discussions with the bewildered employee who has just been demoted or booted clear off the payroll, particularly in these days of "downsizing."

"What did you do that got you fired?" one might ask.

And you might receive a reply like this: "I don't know! I honestly don't know. My performance reviews were all favorable . . . and my boss kept telling me I was doing a good job. Then, all of a sudden, I was fired. I honestly don't know why."

Although it is probably true that some employees pretend ignorance of the reason for their sudden separation, it would be foolish to assume that all of them are being deceitful. More likely it never occurred to anyone to tell the employees what was expected of them; or perhaps those in charge were not mature enough (i.e., no backbone) to inform them of what they were doing to cause the displeasure of the establishment.

Remember when you were in school and the test papers came back? How often have you heard or said, "Gee. He/she never told us that grades were going to be based on the footnotes (or the lab work, or neatness, or any number of other things). If we had known what he/she wanted, we could have done a lot better."

It's easy for invisible expectations to creep into the equation. Jobs change, quality and output expectations change, and often the communication of those changes to those involved is slow to catch up. So always look to see whether performance expectations are known and clearly understood.

Inadequate Resources and Other Obvious Obstacles

Physical obstacles are often not hard to see. If your car won't move, and you discover that the emergency brake is still on, or that a rock is blocking the front wheel, you disengage the brake, move the rock, and get on with life. Same thing in the workplace. Suppose, for example, you find a discrepancy like this:

Who?	Supermarket shelf stockers
Actual performance:	Stocking 100 cases per hour
Desired performance:	Stocking 150 cases per hour

You look around and find that this stocker spends a lot of time walking between the stockroom and the shelves, struggling with one case at a time. A simple question reveals that he lacks a basic tool, namely a dolly that will carry several cases at a time. Provide a dolly and you'll have eliminated a big obstacle to performing as desired, not to mention making the job easier.

The Case of the Tool Crib

Here is another example, taken from life, but with a different kind of obvious obstacle.

Who?	Machinists
Actual performance:	Don't return expensive, specialized tools to the tool crib after use
Desired performance:	Check tools back in when job is completed

Important? Yes. The tools are very expensive, not readily replaced, and in short supply within the shop. Sometimes work is delayed while chasing down a needed tool which is not in its place in the tool crib. Do all concerned know this? Yes. So why don't they follow the rules? Because the tool crib is likely to be temporarily closed when the machinists try to return tools. Seems the person in charge of the crib takes frequent breaks and, like a diligent cribkeeper, locks the crib rather than leave it unattended. The result, however, is that the attempt to return tools is often frustrated. After a few such frustrations, the machinists find they waste less time if they just leave the tools where they are.

———————

Inadequate Feedback

The third place to look for "miracle fixes" is in the area of feedback—information about the quality of performance. If you aren't getting regular information to answer the "How am I doing?" question, you don't have a basis for improving performance. Practice alone, without feedback, is not enough to "make perfect." In fact, performance is as likely to get worse as it is to get better when feedback is absent.

Often, of course, we can generate our own feedback. But that only works once we have learned how to recognize good from bad performance. If you know that in planting a rose the hole needs to be twice the size of the football, then you can decide (that is, provide yourself with feedback) when the hole is big enough. But if, say, you're practicing shooting at a hidden target, with no way of telling where the bullets are flying, how can you improve your aim? Or if nobody, not even you, tastes the food you have prepared, how can you tell whether it needs more salt?

(Pause for thought: When was the last time you received any feedback regarding the quality of your telephone-answering performance? Do you know anyone who needs such feedback?)

The Case of the Dancing Smiles .

Consider this example: A dance coach wants your help in training dancers to smile whenever they're on stage. To observe the situation for yourself, you go to the theater and sit in the fifth row with the coach while the dancers run through their routines.

Who?	Dancers
Actual Performance:	Not smiling when dancing
Desired Performance:	Smiles on dancers' faces

Whenever one of the dancers drops her smile, the coach leans over to you and says, "See? She's not smiling." So you ask, "Why don't you tell that to the dancer you're pointing at?" You're thinking, "It doesn't do the dancers any good if I'm the only one getting the feedback." The coach replies, "I can't do that. Interruptions like that would completely ruin their timing."

So here is a situation in which *you* got feedback, but the *dancers* didn't. They obviously don't need training; they already know how to smile. Apparently, the dancers were concentrating so hard on counting the beat that they forgot to smile. Suppose the coach had them face their mirrored wall as they practiced; then they would be able to see when they were doing things right (when they weren't watching their feet, that is).

NOTE: You say that dealing with dancers isn't a part of your job description? How about other people for whom smiling might be said to be part of the job—receptionists, flight attendants, store clerks; or managers and trainers?

If you need further examples of performance that suffers from lack of feedback, you need look no further than the institution of marriage. If you have ever heard anyone say things such as:

"Every once in awhile she just clams up. She won't talk to me, and she won't tell me what's bothering her."

"Whenever I try to tell him what he did that upset me, he just walks away."

you're listening to situations wherein feedback is being withheld. The clammer-upper is missing an opportunity to communicate (provide feedback), as is he who walks away. Until the situation changes, it will be difficult for the relationship to improve.

When, for whatever reason, people cannot generate feedback for themselves and there's no outside source of feedback for expected performance, you have to expect the desired performance to be less than adequate. Turning that around, always make sure that a feedback source exists for what you or someone else expects people to do.

Summing Up

When an identified performance discrepancy warrants action, we should explore fast fixes before spending time and resources on further analysis. We may find that all that is required is a quick-and-easy remedy such as uncovering invisible expectations, providing proper resources, and supplying feedback.

What to Do

Before plunging into the serious analysis of a discrepancy, check to see whether there are one or more obvious impediments to performance that can be readily eliminated or lessened.

How to Do It

Ask these questions:

- Do the performers know what's expected of them? Have they been told or otherwise notified, or is it assumed that "everybody knows?" Are any written standards incomplete or unclear?

- Can the performers tell you what they're expected to do? To accomplish?

- Are there obvious obstacles to performance? Are all needed tools available? Is something missing or inadequate in the work environment? Do they have everything they're supposed to have for doing their job?

- Do performers find out how well they're doing? How do they find out?

Part III

Are the Consequences Right-Side Up?

*Does desired performance
lead to consequences favorable
to the performers?*

A fertile area for clues about how to fix the problem is that
of performance consequences. Because upside-down consequences are such a common source of the problem, they
should be addressed before moving to more familiar causes.

4

Is Desired Performance Punishing?

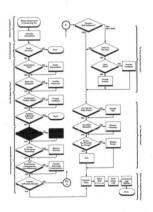

WHERE WE ARE

An important discrepancy in someone's performance needs to be eliminated. We need to check to see whether desired performance is being punished.

Actions lead to results. Sit on a hot stove, and the consequence of doing so will make it much less likely that you'll do it again. Recognize someone's good work with attention or favorable comments, and it's more likely that the person will continue to do good work.

Actions produce consequences; those consequences, favorable or unfavorable, shape how we will act in the future. Favorable consequences make it more likely that actions will be repeated. Unfavorable consequences work the other way, decreasing the likelihood of repeated performance. We need to be sure that this linkage of actions and consequences is not working against us, with punishing consequences following desired actions.

The last thing we want to do is to punish good performance. Yet strange to say, one of the most common reasons why people don't do what we'd like them to do is that the desired "doing" is seen as punishing by the performer(s). Their world becomes somehow dimmer as a result of what they did, and so they seek (consciously and otherwise) other ways to go. Here are several examples we've encountered over the years.

Actual Cases

The following real cases demonstrate how desired performance can be punishing.

A Case of Musical Madness

A college music student had the chance to play with his city's symphony orchestra. For a student who had not yet completed his training, this was a rare opportunity. Since he needed both the money and the experience, he asked his music teacher if something could be worked out.

"I think so," replied the teacher. "There is no reason why you shouldn't take the job, provided you make up the school work you miss on the days you are absent."

So, the student threw himself into both tasks. He did well with the symphony and earned "As" and "Bs" on all his make-up work. But when grading time arrived, he found himself with a "C" for the course. Astonished, he asked his teacher why he was given only a "C" after receiving "As" and "Bs" for all his work.

She replied: "Well, you're getting entirely too much experience and not enough learning."

If you were the student, how would you feel in such a situation? No matter how you slice it, this is a situation in which desirable activity was followed by an unpleasant consequence (punishment). If, as a result of this dampening, the student were to perform his school work with less enthusiasm, one can imagine the teacher telling her colleagues, "You know, we've got to teach him to be more motivated about his studies. He oughta wanna have more interest."

A Case of Attitude

Some time ago one of us was assigned the task of "fixing the doctors' attitudes" at a large hospital. The hospital had just installed a computer, and physicians were now expected to *type* their medical orders into a terminal twice a day, instead of scribbling them on a pad.

"But they're not doing that," explained management. "Instead, they're grumbling about it, doing it wrong, or trying to get the nurses to do it for them." Asked, "Why should the physicians do it willingly?" management replied, "Because it's good for the hospital—and for the patient. The labs get the medication orders a lot faster, inventory can be kept up more easily, and the billing is more accurate."

In other words, lots of good consequences for the hospital, but what about the physicians? For the physicians, desired performance was punishing—in spades.

After two days of on-site observation, here is what was found. The terminals had been placed in the nursing stations—very busy, public, and crowded places. As a result, there was no place to put a piece of paper down to the left or right of a terminal; and as each terminal top was "modern-designed" to slope downward, any paper placed there would slither to the floor. Now, physicians tend not to be a typing population. Some type competently, but most don't; and many think of typing as somewhat demeaning "clerk's work." The result was that most physicians would sit at terminals, notes in one hand, with the "proctological" finger of the other hand laboriously "hunting 'n' pecking" away at their medical orders.

The nurses, who had banded together to agree not to take over this chore, would tend to stand in the background and snicker. After all, they typed on the terminals regularly and were pretty good at it.

There's more. The terminals were mounted on tables 30 inches high. That's no problem for you with your perfect vision, but those of us who wear bifocals find ourselves sitting at terminals with our heads tilted back and our necks getting stiff. The same thing happened to many of the physicians. Had you observed them you would have noticed that after a short while of sitting with heads bent back, some would (unconsciously, it seemed) slide out of their seats, push the chairs to the tables, and then look *down* at the screens. This was far more comfortable for the necks and eyes, but action led to yet another source of punishment. When they picked up light pens to touch the screens and thus enter their orders into the computer, they sometimes hit the "Erase" spot rather than the "Enter" spot and wiped out all their hard work. You see, the computer programmer had put the "Enter" code on the screen right next to the "Erase."

Finally, to add insult to injury, because the physicians were looking *down* at the computer screen at an angle (because they were standing rather than sitting), they were likely to touch *another* wrong place with their light pens because of the parallax problem (the bending of light by the thickness of the glass screen, much as water bends light and makes a partially submerged stick look bent), and get whooshed to the other end of the program.

Adding it all up, desired performance (typing orders into a computer terminal) was mildly painful, humiliating, frustrating, and exasperating. Should anyone be surprised that there was some grumbling and a reluctance to perform as requested?

The solution was simple. Two terminals were installed on low tables in the physicians' office complex. There, each physician could enter medical orders at his or her convenience, in private and in relative comfort.

The Case of the Reluctant Readers

Examples of instances in which desired performance is punished are everywhere, but sometimes the source(s) of punishment are less visible than in the examples above.

"Trainees just won't read the material they are assigned before coming to the course," instructors will complain.

But why should they? What happens to them if they *do?* Well, the instructor goes over the same material anyhow, thus creating a boring time for those who did as requested.

What happens to the trainees who *don't* do the reading? Nothing. The reading is covered anyway. So desired performance is punishing, and undesired performance is largely ignored. Is it any wonder people don't do the reading assignments? Listen to this story.

A Case of Welfare Woes

In one welfare office the supervisors complained that social workers were closing fewer cases than they should.

"Not everyone stays on welfare for generations," a supervisor explained. "Social workers should be helping people to establish objectives and to accomplish them, and then the workers should close those cases."

But consider the consequences to the *social workers* who did what was expected of them. If they *closed* cases, they had, in their own words, to open other cases. And that took a lot of legwork until each case "settled down." By "settle down" they meant that in time, cases usually become routine and can be handled with periodic phone calls or visits. In other words, the consequence of desired performance was more work.

What happened to them if they *didn't* close cases? The supervisors complained . . . among *themselves*. Why? Because the supervisors preferred that their social workers produce fat reports with lots of psychiatric language, rather than good records for closing cases.

The Case of the Reluctant Manager

An insurance company had a policy of trying to recruit upper-level managers from the ranks of its field agencies. But the agency managers resisted the promotions. One of them described the situation this way:

"They tell me it would be good *for the company* if I accepted the promotion and moved to corporate headquarters back East. But why would I want to do that? The raise doesn't mean that much. Besides, I'm my own boss here. I do the hiring and firing; I set the working hours. I know everybody in town; I belong to the club and play golf with my friends. Why should I give up all this just to sit in a concrete blockhouse back East?"

From this agency manager's point of view, the performance desired by head-office management (accepting the promotion) would definitely make his world dimmer. And if a consequence makes someone's world dimmer, less pleasant, or less interesting, you can consider that a punishing consequence. In this example not only was desired performance punishing, but *non*-performance (staying on as agency manager) was highly rewarding. In situations such as these, it is folly to expect that "inspirational lectures" or exhortation will do much good.

The Case of the Empowerment Trap

In these days when empowerment of the workforce is such a popular business practice, it is common for managers to "empower" employees to make decisions and take actions previously reserved for managers. So far, so good. Unfortunately, however, the empowered employees aren't told specifically what they are empowered to do now that they weren't empowered to do yesterday. As a result, they are reluctant to behave any differently than before the empowerment policy went into effect.

In addition, managers themselves sometimes get no training in how to handle this new-style management. In particular, they don't get information and practice in dealing with employees who *do* behave as they're expected to. The result? Employees who behave in the expected empowered ways can get dumped on by managers who don't know how to recognize empowered actions when they see them. Would you be surprised to learn that "punishment for empowered behavior" often leads to less of it?

Consequences Work at Home, Too

Punishment for desired or superior performance is so common that one may overlook it in an area where it frequently occurs—the family. Yet punishment is plain to see in what we call the "anti-intellectual family." Think about the consequence to sons or daughters who aspire to rise above the intellectual level of their relatives, or who set their sights on occupations different from those pursued by relatives, or who raise their conversations above the level of the family "norm." Are they applauded or revered or urged to greater heights? Seldom. More likely, they are insulted and stung with ridicule so that they lose their motivation to escape their mental ghettos.

In many more cases around the home, desired performance is withheld because of its unfavorable consequence. Parents complain, "I don't know what they teach 'em in school these days, but our kids don't come to us with their questions and problems like they used to." Observe these same parents interacting with their children, however, and it quickly becomes apparent that the parents are causing the problem.

> *Kid:* Hey, Mom 'n' Dad! Look what I made in school today!
>
> *Parent:* Wipe ... your ... mouth!

Little wonder the kids behave as they do. The parents, unintentionally perhaps, have engineered it that way. And usually they couldn't have done a better job if they had been trying.

These examples are here to remind you of a simple truth about human behavior:

People learn to avoid the things they are hit with!

It doesn't matter whether they are hit with a club, an insult, humiliation, repeated failure, frustration, boredom, or an increased workload of uninteresting tasks. If people feel they will be punished, or even that there is a risk of being punished when they perform as you desire, they will avoid doing it your way whenever they can. People don't often purposely do things that will lead to their world being dimmer than it is.

Spotting Ill-Placed Punishment

A classic example from industry is the comparative empha-sis on safety and production. Management says, "Safety is our top priority. Right after it comes productivity."

But what does a supervisor's reputation depend upon? Pro-duction. You'll rarely hear, "Great supervisor. Tremendous safety record. This is the person we'll promote."

Safety managers complain that as long as nothing goes wrong—as long as people "get away with it"—nobody cares about safety.

Production is seen as the result that counts. And despite the lip service, safety takes a second (or third or fourth) seat in the perception of those affected.

And so, when people aren't performing as desired, one thing to explore is whether or not it is unnecessarily punishing to perform as desired. Do they see desired performance as being geared to penalties? If so, you have probably located a strong reason why you aren't getting the results you would like.

We must emphasize, however, that it is not *your* view of the outcome that is important here. You must try to see the situation through the eyes of the performers themselves and ask yourself, "What is the result to them for doing as I desire? How might *they* see the consequences of doing it?" What may strike you as a favorable consequence could be seen as *un*favorable by them.

On occasion, this can be subtle. Sometimes it may strike you as ridiculous. No matter. Listen to what the performers say.

The employer complains, "I don't see why they won't work overtime—they make good money on it." But the employees say, "What's the good of overtime? Anything you earn, they take away in taxes."

The parent says, "I don't see why she won't take math. It will get her a better job when she's grown." But the student says, "Math is for those who want to follow the establishment road. I'm interested in *people*. Besides, the math teacher is the least liked guy in the whole school."

Or consider the case of "rate busters" in school or industry—those who turn out more work than anyone else. Do colleagues revere these people for their skill or industriousness? More likely, the group's attitude will be perceived as punishment for performance, and the person will slow down to the level of the group . . . or be pushed out of it.

ann landers

Dear Ann Landers: I have never written to you before but after I read the letter signed "Lonesome" I knew my time had come.

My in-laws are also "Lonesome"—or at least that's what they tell everybody.

We hear from many people that they complain constantly about how we ignore them and how hurt they are. It burns me up.

Last Sunday my husband and I and the kids went to see them and it was the same old story.

Grandma and Grandpa talked about nothing but how sick they are, how much they suffer (she with backaches and he with rheumatism in his legs). It is a real contest to see who is in worse shape.

Then they tell us for the 50th time about how bad their operations were. (Hers two years ago for a tumor, his five years ago for a hernia.)

They are so self-centered it is awful. Never a question about the children or my husband's job or my interests.

All they want to do is talk about themselves and their sicknesses.

Also, whenever we go to see them they greet us with, "We didn't think you were coming."

I wonder how many other "Lonesome" parents there are around? If so, maybe there's a good reason their children don't visit them more often. —Cause and Effect

Dear Cause: There are plenty around, and I hear from dozens of them. Your signature was most appropriate.

Whenever you get an "effect" like the one described in your letter there's got to be a "cause." Thanks for writing.

Did you ever attend a school where the consequence of knowing your subject or of showing your intelligence was ridicule from other students? Where the "in" thing was not to do homework and not to make good grades? Where diligent students were dismissed as "nerds," "eggheads," and "brains," or worse? (By the way, so far as we know, *all* the terms used by students to describe their diligent colleagues are disparaging or insulting.)

Or consider the eight-year-old girl who avoided playing with kids her age, preferring to hang around with adults. Why? Because to the adults she was intelligent, smart, creative, and well-behaved. She felt accepted. What happened when she played with kids her own age (the desired performance)? She was made fun of because of her haircut, her weight, her eyeglasses, her failure at sports, and because she excelled at her school work. Upside-down consequences are everywhere.

You hear teachers and administrators complain of students who don't do their homework. "They oughta wanna do their homework. If they don't, they will be doomed to a lifetime of mediocrity." And then, because teachers and administrators fail to look at the problem from the students' viewpoint, they make new policies that only aggravate the situation.

This can be doubly punishing for the students. They perceive homework first as an onerous duty that replaces more pleasant activities. If, despite this, they do the homework, the lumps they take from their peers may outweigh more positive outcomes, such as good grades and teacher approval. So next time, they don't do their homework. So the school invents new punitive policies, and more threat of failure is laid on. Now the students perceive yet another reason to beat the system. (One can't help thinking of two gladiators beating each other to death with bloodied clubs, each telling the other he oughta wanna be the first to stop.)

The situation is even worse when homework is used as the actual instrument of punishment. It goes like this: "All right! Just for *that* you can do *fifty* math problems for homework rather than the ten I was *going* to assign!" When you punish others that way, you may leave them hating the very thing you want them to "learn to love."

A more effective way to break the miserable chain of events would be to make the consequence of studying more immediately favorable than it currently is, so that those who study successfully will have reason to be envied rather than ridiculed. Rather than complain that students "oughta wanna" study *for their own good,* make desired privileges dependent upon the performance wanted.

More Actual Cases

The following cases demonstrate additional ways that desired performance can be punishing.

The Case of the Dental Dance

Several years ago the clinical faculty of a dental school complained that students were putting in too little laboratory time on dentures they were making for their patients. The situation was this. Students treated their patients in the clinic. When adjustments were needed in the fitting of dentures, the student would go to the laboratory to make adjustments and then return to the patient in the clinic to try again. The complaint of the faculty was that the students were not as painstaking as they should have been and as they knew how to be in getting dentures to fit. "We've got to teach them to be less careless," was the cry. "We've got to teach them to have the right attitude." (What would they put in such a curriculum—molar appreciation?)

When the question, "What is the consequence of performing correctly?" was finally asked, the nature of the problem became obvious. The laboratory was one floor up and at the other end of the building from the clinic. Obviously, it was less punishing to cut a few corners than to run up and down every few minutes. When the lab was finally moved next to the clinic, the quality of the dentures improved miraculously—without any added instruction or exhortation—and the faculty ceased to complain about students' attitudes toward dentures.

The Case of the Call-Button Caper

The hospital provides another example of how it is possible to design *against* the results one wants. Patients who cannot get out of bed have a call button with which to summon help. Mostly, the system works quite well. Occasionally, however, a patient will resist pressing the call button for long periods of time even though in great distress.

Why would a patient not press the call button when he or she is in need? What consequence of pressing might cause the patient to suffer? Is it possible that button-pushing can be punishing?

You bet it can! It can be embarrassing, even upsetting. Occasionally, pushing the button summons a grouch who bursts into the room with a "What now?" or a "Not *you* again?" After only a few such experiences, the weakened patient finds it easier to tolerate distress than to press the "Help" button.

A Case of Unsafe Safety

Industry, too, has its situations in which desired performance is punishing. For example, the flouting of safety regulations despite "safety training" is a familiar problem. Though people know how to recognize and report a safety hazard, often they don't. Why not? It may not be safe.

In some places, reporting safety hazards is looked on as "rocking the boat." (It usually implies that someone has been sloppy or irresponsible.) In others, it's considered "chicken" to use protective goggles or a saw guard. Regardless of the reason, the consequence of hazard reporting is punishment. The person reporting may be looked down on or insulted by peers and may have to bear the brunt of insults. Sometimes, the "rules" of the department may even be "explained" with a fist. It's not unheard of for someone to be fired for calling attention to hazards—after being accused of "whistleblowing," of course!

When a problem arises because performance is punishing, plainly the answer is not the usual "Train 'em." Desirable consequences have to follow desirable performance. Better solutions have included recognition, even bonuses, to individuals and departments with good safety records.

A Case of Meeting Madness

For another common, if less important, example, take meeting-attending behavior. Time is wasted waiting for latecomers. But late-coming persists no matter how often instructions are given or exhortations are delivered. Plainly, this isn't a miniature training problem. To get at the true problem, you have to ask: "What's the conse-quence of performing as desired?"

What happens if you arrive *on time?* Well, you have to sit around and wait for latecomers. That can be punishing, especially if you have work to do.

What's the result of being *late?* The meeting starts almost as soon as you arrive.

Thus, punctuality is punished and tardiness is rewarded, precisely the opposite of what is intended. The solution is to reverse the "polar-ity" of the consequences; make it rewarding to be on time, and pun-ishing to be late. How? Here are some suggestions:

- Start the meeting on time.
- Make something pleasant happen at the start of the meeting.
- Present information at the start of the meeting that the late-comers will miss.
- Hand out the plum assignments at the start of the meeting.
- Save less attractive assignments for the latecomers.

The Case of the Reluctant Loaners

Another interesting problem of this sort arose when a bank decided, "We've got to teach our branch managers to be a little less conservative about making loans." The remainder of the conversation with management went like this:

"Do these managers know how to be riskier about making loans?"

"Yes. They merely have to accept those loan applications closest to the top of the reject pile."

"Do they know you want them to be less conservative?"

"Oh, yes. We have been sending them corporate memos for the past six months, but it doesn't seem to do much good."

"What happens to managers who take a conservative stance?"

"All their loans are paid back and they are looked at favorably by their superiors."

"What happens if they take the riskier stance, as desired?"

"Well, if some of their loans default, their superiors rate their performances down."

The Case of the Reluctant Tellers

Another example of the double-bind of upside-down consequences, again from the world of banking: Tellers were urged to sell the bank's extra services, such as special accounts and rentals of safe-deposit boxes. At the same time, the tellers were expected to keep the lines of waiting customers short. Since service-selling takes time, it tends to keep the lines longer. As long lines are more visible and their consequences more immediate than the selling or non-selling of services, service-selling tends to get the short end of the pickle.

Or consider this common situation:

> *Mgr:* That's right, boss. It wasn't easy, but I managed to get my division in $50,000 under budget this year.
>
> *Boss:* (Beaming.) That's great! Now I can reduce your budget by that amount for next year.

Notice what's happening here. Two different people are reading the same event in different ways. For bosses, coming in under budget is rewarding. For managers, a cut in next year's budget may be perceived as anything but rewarding. Bosses who want to encourage getting under budget need to pump some sunshine toward their managers, not kick them in the financial butt.

Perception is important here. Whenever people aren't doing what they should be doing, look for consequences that the *performer* sees as punishing. Eliminating or diminishing the sources of that punishment will make it more likely that people will perform as desired.

Summing Up

When faced with a performance discrepancy, suspect that, no matter what else may be contributing to the problem, desired performance is being punished.

Upside-down consequences, beating people down when they should be built up, are common. When you find such negative (aversive) effects, eliminate them or reduce their effect and do all you can to create or strengthen positive or desired consequences. And be sure that those new consequences are considered favorable by the performers.

As we said, people learn to avoid the things they are hit with.

What to Do

Determine whether desired performance leads to unfavorable consequences.

How to Do It

Ask these questions:

- What is the consequence of performing as desired?

- Is it punishing to perform as expected?

- Does the person perceive desired performance as being geared to penalties?

- Would the person's world become dimmer by doing it the expected way?

5
Is Undesired Performance Rewarding?

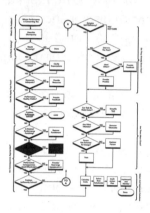

WHERE WE ARE

We are dealing with a discrepancy needing elimination, and we want to know whether the "wrong" or undesired performance accidentally leads to one or more forms of reward.

In the last chapter, we examined the fact that sometimes people don't do what they're expected to do because doing it the expected way leads to unpleasant results.

There is another side to this issue. Performance may not be as expected because some other way of performing is actually *rewarding*. That is, whether or not desired performance has favorable consequences, they are not as favorable as those of an *other*-than-desired performance. Thus, another place to look for causes of undesired performance is in the consequences of that undesired performance. In other words, find out what happens *to them* when they don't do it the way they're expected to do it.

Actual Cases

Here are some examples of situations in which undesirable performance was rewarding—where doing it "wrong" led to more favorable consequences than doing it "right."

A Case of Preventive Maintenance

An office equipment manufacturer maintains a large staff of people whose task it is to repair customers' equipment when it goes belly-up. Their work is usually satisfactory, but at one point, management noticed what was said to be a performance discrepancy.

"They just aren't doing their pm's," they said. A "pm" is a preventive-maintenance routine involving dusting, adjusting, oiling, and replacement of suspiciously worn parts.

"We've sent them several memos, but they just don't do a pm when they should—which is every time they service a machine," said management.

It was puzzling, especially since "doing a pm" was good for the machine, good for company image, and thus good for sales, and even good for the maintenance people. (pm's helped avoid the embarrassment of repeat calls.) The source of the problem was revealed when questions were asked about consequences.

"What happens if they *don't* do their pm's?" Well, the machine works just as well as it would otherwise, for the moment, and the service call takes less time.

"What happens if they *do* the pm as desired?" Well, then the service call takes a little longer. And though top management wanted the pm's done, the service managers were evaluating performance mainly by counting the number of minutes spent on a service call. So to do the pm's (the desired performance) was to risk losing out on pay raises and promotions.

Remedy? Find one or more ways to make undesired performance (NOT doing pm's) less rewarding than doing them. This was done by describing the accomplishments expected of the technicians and then rewarding them for the quality of the service calls. This meant, among other things, rewarding them more highly for service calls that didn't require callbacks (repeat visits to correct earlier mistakes or things overlooked) rather than for the time taken to complete the call.

A Case of "I Don't Make the Rules"

Examples of people performing in ways that are other than desirable are not hard to find. There's the maternity ward receptionist who makes you fill out a dozen documents when it's obvious that the arrival of your child is imminent, and there's the emergency room receptionist who makes you provide documentation proving that you're rich enough to pay, even though it's obvious that you are bleeding to death or that your nose is about to fall off. Then there's the petty bureaucrat who counters all of your attempts to get something done with a regulation that says you can't, but who never offers a hint of the right course to follow.

If you take the view that these people are supposed to facilitate rather than obstruct, you have to conclude that they are performing in an undesirable manner. Obstructive behavior must be more rewarding than facilitating behavior, probably because of the "attention" they get from their frustrated petitioners for the former, even though the formal rewards of the job (pay, promotions) are apparently tied to the latter.

Push back at one of these functionaries and you will quickly be told, "I'm just doing my job. I don't make the rules."

Some of these misguided souls, finding no other satisfaction in their work, get satisfaction (attention?) from exerting petty tyranny over others. Others may be speaking the literal but partial truth when they say, "I'm just doing my job." They should add for the sake of accuracy," . . . in a way that I perceive that my superiors want it done." Their perceptions may be far from accurate.

In all cases, something positive can be done. For petty tyrants, one has to find a way to make their world brighter when they perform in the desired way. (And since this may be hard to do, one may have to fall back on the last-but-not-least alternative: Change the job or change the person.) For those who have an inaccurate picture of what their superiors want, there's plainly a need to spell out the true intent—ensuring that they know what is to be done and can recognize when it has been done properly.

A Case of Keeping Subordinates Uninformed

Here's a similar example: "We've got to teach Mary to train her staff." (It's the production manager of a manufacturing company speaking about one of the "leads.") "Training is her responsibility."

The lead knew what her people needed to know, all right, but didn't tell them, so production suffered.

Why didn't she do what needed to be done? What did she get out of keeping her staff ignorant?

Status! Anyone who wanted to know what was going on had to talk to her. The lead saw herself as the queen bee. Keeping subordinates uninformed, she thought she would keep things that way. It was more rewarding not to perform as expected.

Solution? Not training. Make it *matter* to perform as desired.

The Case of All Is Not Gold

In one of the large gold mines of Africa, the management once decided that they had a training problem involving African underground workers who operated the drilling rigs on the mine face. "We've got to teach these men to wear their earplugs," they said. The discussion with one of the managers went something like this:

"What happens if these men don't wear their earplugs?"

"Why, they go stone deaf from the unbelievable noise."

"Do they know that they're expected to wear earplugs?"

"Of course they do."

"Do they know *how* to wear their earplugs?"

"Of course. All they have to do is stick them into their ears."

"Do they have the plugs handy?"

"Yes. They carry them in their pockets. In fact, they are checked when they enter the mine to make sure they *do* have their earplugs with them."

"I see. So they know how to wear the plugs, and the plugs are always available?"

"That's right. But they don't wear them, and they really should."

"Why?"

"Why, to keep from going deaf, of course."

"Do you have any idea why they *don't* wear their earplugs?"

"You know why they don't wear their earplugs? They don't wear their earplugs because this is the highest job an African can have in this mine . . . and he wears his deafness like a *status symbol.*"

Well, that put a new light on the problem. Then it was seen for what it was, a problem where performing as desired wasn't nearly as rewarding as performing otherwise. Loss of hearing was more desirable than loss of status. Notice again that all the training in the world is not likely to get those earplugs worn.

And before you conclude that this example is cultural, think about all the people who would rather suffer pain or disfigurement for similar status reasons: women of the world who suffer pain from shoes that are too tight, the millions who risk disease and early death rather than quit smoking, athletes who continue playing with painful injuries rather than sit on the sidelines. And what about those who endure pain or ill health because they believe they are avoiding even greater pain— those who endure a painful toothache rather than go to a dentist, or chance getting measles or mumps rather than tolerate the needle in a simple inoculation?

No doubt you can think of several possible solutions if the problem is posed this way: How can we make "being a driller" more visible to the outside world than deafness? Give them a special uniform? Stripes on their sleeves, or gold braid on a cap? Some symbol, like the physician's stethoscope, to hang around their necks?

Not as Rare as You Might Think

Situations like this aren't as rare as you might think. Though you may think it "unbelievable" that people would rather go deaf than wear earplugs, you can find similar examples if you just look around you.

The Case of Old Leatherlung

In working with a group of firefighters on performance analysis issues, we learned of this little gem:

"They're supposed to wear their breathing apparatus when they go into a hot fire, but often they don't."

"What happens if they wear it, as they're supposed to?"

"Well, they complain that it's heavy, hard to see through the eyepieces, and clumsy to work with."

"And what happens if they don't wear the breathing apparatus?"

"If they don't wear it they have more mobility and can see better. And if they don't wear it, and live, they get to be known as 'old leatherlung', and that's real hero stuff."

Clearly that was a case where undesirable performance (not wearing the apparatus) was more rewarding than performing as desired. Keep in mind that people respond to consequences whether they are aware of them or not. In other words, in most instances people don't *deliberately* non-perform. They simply do it because their world is more comfortable or pleasant that way than it is if they do it the way someone else says is the desired way.

It's a fact that there's a whole world out there just filled with people who are not doing as you would like. Not all are acting against your wishes because they don't know any better or because they don't know how to do differently. Most behave the way they do because they feel that *their* way leads to more favorable consequences for them than does *your* way. If you want them to do differently, you will have to invent an approach where doing it right feels better than doing it their way.

This is an appropriate point to note that problems of this kind do not always fall so neatly into categories (desired performance punished; undesirable performance rewarded) as do our examples. Typically, problems have elements of more than one of the categories we have discussed, or they can move from one category to another.

In this chapter we have looked at cases where the consequences of *un*desired performance were more favorable than those that followed desired performance. Now consider this case.

The Case of "Ol' Boney"

"Our department has a dozen truck drivers. They're all safe drivers, except one, and he costs about two thousand dollars per year in property damage and ill will. We never know when he's going to hit somebody. And he's also erratic in his private driving, as his record shows. He's run over a gas pump, run over a customer's wet concrete, and so on."

"Is it a skill deficiency, do you think?"

"No, because most months his driving is perfect."

"Hmm. What happens when he does have an accident?"

"Then he gets a lot of attention from his cronies. They gather around him and ask him to recount the episode while they chuckle. 'Ol' Boney's done it again,' they'll say, and he gets to tell it again."

"By the way, what happens to your good drivers?"

"What do you mean?"

"What is the consequence of having a good driving record?"

"We don't do anything special for good drivers; that's what we expect of them."

"Oh."

Even our educational establishment is loaded with examples of conditions or consequences that make someone's world brighter for *not* performing as you wish.

Water the What?

Let's begin with an analogy. Suppose that while walking in the park you come upon a man standing in front of two plants and muttering to himself. He is using a watering can to water one of the plants. You ask him what he is doing.

"I'm trying to make *that* one grow," he replies, and points to the *other* one.

"Well," you might ask, puzzled, "if you want *that* one to grow, why are you watering *this* one?"

"Because the other one oughta wanna grow anyhow! It's the plantlike thing to do."

Wacky? Of course. Yet this is very much like the way our school system is operated.

The chief goal of a school is alleged to be to help students' capabilities grow—to change their state of knowledge, skill, and understanding. Thus, the measure of success is the degree to which the students' capabilities are increased. Since student performance is what is desired, one would think that the rewards of the system (money, raises, position, status) would be strongly tied to teaching excellence. Yet this appears not to be the case. Look at the salary schedule of nearly every school and you will find that the rewards (favorable consequences) of the system have little direct relationship to effective teaching. Raises and promotions are based almost exclusively on the number of months served and the number of academic credit hours earned. There is as yet little or no attempt to tie these rewards for the teacher to the quantity and quality of student performance.

In these circumstances, to say that teachers oughta wanna teach more effectively is to behave like the nut with the watering can—it is demanding one kind of performance while rewarding another. (To improve the situation, of course, would require examining the forces that are opposed to judging teachers on the basis of their ability to teach.)

The situation is even more bizarre at the university level. Here, professors get promotions and raises not on how well they succeed with students, but on the basis of how much they publish, how many government grants they are able to garner, and the number of committees on which they serve. Again, they are exhorted to do one thing while being rewarded for another.

Since people tend to do those things that brighten their world, the moral is:

Water the performance you want to grow.

Think for a moment about the expression "resistance to change." It's a judgment often made about people who don't perform as desired. But the expression is misleading, because it puts a derogatory emphasis where it doesn't belong. When people oppose the introduction of some new idea or thing, there usually isn't an *active* resistance in force. Often, people cling to the old because there is *no real reason,* no favorable consequence to *them,* for doing it the new way. It is more comfortable, more pleasant, more rewarding to stay with the old. So here again, simply plying people with information about the new thing or exhorting them that they oughta wanna be in favor of newness may not change much. The desired performance (the new thing) will be more readily adopted (and made to work during any "teething troubles") if it is plain to the doer how it will make his or her world brighter.

In much the same way, the teacher passes the blame for his or her own failure to be interesting by complaining about students' "short attention spans." It would be much better if he or she approached the problem by asking, "What's the consequence to the student who *does* pay attention?" If the honest answer is "boredom," then there isn't much doubt where the remedy lies.

One more type of situation. Let's call it the "don't-let's-stick-our-necks-out-more-than-we-have-to" category. It's found at many levels in the working world and in private life, and can be found under at least two subheadings—the mental version and the physical version.

A typical instance of the first is found in people who apparently "don't like to take responsibility." These are often people who have discovered that when they make a wrong decision, they get it in the neck. And if they get it in the neck often enough and hard enough, they're going to conclude that one way of shutting off aversive consequences is to make *fewer* of these decisions. Eventually, they establish an equilibrium, making as few decisions as it is possible to make without getting genuine complaints that they're loafing.

You can think of your own examples of students who try but get poor grades, and children who seem reluctant to do chores.

That's the mental aspect of the problem. The physical aspect is similar. Some activities are physically exacting; the more a person does, the more tired he or she gets. When getting excessively tired leads to no positive consequence, the doer finds a point of equilibrium.

When someone is exhibiting these symptoms, mental or physical, people may say, "He's a good man, but. . . ." Or, leaping sprightly to conclusions, they judge: "She's not ambitious." "He doesn't care." "She procrastinates." Or worst of all, "He's lazy."

The people judged may not like to act this way. But, as they see the world, the less they do, the less they have to answer for or the less they suffer. The consequence—or, more accurately in most cases, the sum of the consequences—for doing more is not worth the effort.

Maybe they don't have the mental or physical stuff to perform as you would like. But if you're the one in charge of the consequences that come to them as a result of action or nonaction, maybe you should take a close look at those consequences to make sure they are worthy of the effort you are expecting.

Summing Up

The cause of the performance discrepancy may be the favorable consequences that follow undesired performance. If the analysis reveals that poor performance is being rewarded, the incentives for performing poorly must be removed.

What to Do

Determine whether undesired performance or other performance leads to more favorable consequences than desired performance does.

How to Do It

Ask these questions:

- What is the result of doing it the present way instead of my way?

- What does the person get out of the present performance in the way of reward, prestige, status, comfort?

- Does the person get more attention for undesirable rather than for desirable performance (for misbehaving than for behaving)?

- What event in the world supports (rewards) the present way of doing things? (Are irrelevant behaviors inadvertently rewarded while crucial behaviors are overlooked?)

- Is this person "mentally inadequate," doing less so that there is less to worry about?

- Is this person "physically inadequate," doing less because it is less tiring or less painful?

6

Are There Any Consequences at All?

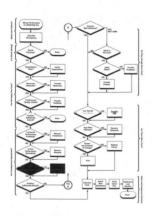

WHERE WE ARE

We are analyzing a performance discrepancy worth doing something about, and want to know whether appropriate consequences are in place.

Sometimes a performance discrepancy continues to exist, not because the consequences of performing are upside-down, but because it simply makes no difference whether people perform or not. There are no meaningful consequences to *them* if they take the trouble to perform, and no consequences to them if they don't.

The laws of nature tell us that unless a performance is followed at least periodically by an event considered favorable by the performer, that performance tends to disappear. Saying it another way, if there is no consequence to make something worth doing, it will tend not to get done.

An important point (because few people seem to grasp it): Wagging your forefinger at someone and telling him or her, "You oughta wanna," does *not* qualify as a universal incentive to action.

A common instance of a performance that dwindles in the absence of a consequence comes from the chore known as paperwork. Managers complain, "Reports just don't get in on time," or "Those reports are haphazardly done." In such instances, the conversation often tends to go like this:

"The reports are sloppily done?"

"They certainly are. And they don't come in on time."

"Why not, do you suppose?"

"Staff members just don't seem to care!"

"What happens if the reports are late?"

"Well, then I have to explain to my superiors why I am late with *my* reports."

"No, no. What happens *to the people who submit the reports?*"

"Well, nothing, I guess. But they oughta wanna get them in on time."

"What happens if the reports are sloppily done?"

"Disaster! My poor secretary works like mad trying to get them cleaned up in time to attach to my own report."

"Yes, of course. But what happens to the people who send in the sloppy work?"

"Well, nothing, I guess."

"You don't phone them or drop them a memo to tell them they have not met expected standards?"

"No."

"You don't send the reports back for *them* to correct?"

"Heavens, no. There's never *time.*"

"So it doesn't really matter *to the staff members* whether their reports are well done and on time?"

"No, I guess not. But they oughta wanna do them right."

Let's not get caught up in a debate about the importance of paperwork. The point is that you're less likely to see desired performance when that performance does not "matter" to the performer—that is, when the performance does not lead to consequences considered favorable by the performer.

Actual Cases

The following cases demonstrate discrepancies when there are no consequences for either good or bad performance.

The Case of the Bopping Sticks

Police departments seem to be as good a source of "no-consequence" examples as business and industry. In one department, patrol teams were required to take their batons (bopping sticks) with them whenever they got out of the patrol car. Apparently this wasn't happening all the time, and so the captain asked the trainer to add something to the instruction that would "teach patrol officers to have the right attitude" about baton handling.

The officers, however, already *knew* they were to take their batons with them. So why didn't they do it? Well, a baton is a stiff, hard item that can cause pain if not removed from the belt ring before entering a patrol car (or any other car, for that matter). As a result, there is a tendency to remove the baton from the belt ring and place it on the seat. On leaving a car, officers may have to take their hats, a clipboard, or perhaps a shotgun, and once in a while there is a tendency to forget the batons.

But consider the consequences to the officers. If they took their batons with them (the desired performance), what happened to them? Nothing much. They had them when they needed them, but that was seldom. What happened if they left them in the car most of the time? Nothing much. Besides, if the radio call described a situation that sounded like a potential head-thumper, they didn't forget to take them along. So there were no consequences for the desired performance either way.

The solution? Well, if it is truly important that batons be in their rings whenever police officers step out of a patrol car, management can inform officers of the expectation and then provide a variety of demerits (that would be recorded on personnel records) for instances in which they are observed to be "out of uniform." Can you think of other possible remedies?

A Clean Case of Dirty Cars

In yet another department, drivers were expected to keep their own patrol cars clean. Because of the "hassle," though, they weren't too diligent about that chore, and management would periodically complain and tack memos onto the bulletin board. When the performance expectation was looked at in terms of consequences, though, favorable responses were again lacking. If drivers went to the trouble of keeping the cars clean, nobody said anything. If the drivers didn't, management nagged. As most people learn to tune out nagging, it hardly qualifies as a meaningful consequence. Without consequences, why should anyone expect the performance to be different from what it is?

The solution to this "problem" was simple. The police department contracted with a local car wash to clean patrol cars whenever they appeared. Drivers were told to run through the car wash whenever they had a little spare time. As that was easy to do, the problem was solved.

The Case of Taking Orders—or Not

In this next example, a manager is discussing the people who work at the serving window of a fast-food chain.

"When taking orders, these window people are supposed to ask whether the customer wants any of the various extras. But most of the time they forget."

"What's the result?"

"The result is that our sales are less than they might be, and customers aren't reminded about items they may really want."

"Yes, but what's the result to the *window people*? What happens to *them* if they forget to tout the extras?"

"Well, we can't afford to stand over their shoulders and tell them every time they forget."

"Does anything *ever* happen to them when they don't do as you want?"

"No, I guess not."

No consequence for doing it right, and none for doing it wrong—and thus, no real urgency for behaving differently. Solution? List all the possible ways of making the order-takers' world a little brighter when performing as desired. Then select one or more that are practical and less expensive than the problem and that would also be seen as favorable by the recipients of the consequence(s).

The Case of You Really Oughta Wanna Sit Down Front

And here's a common "problem" solved by ingenuity. A professor kept urging his students to "sit down front" when attending lectures in the tiered classroom, but students continued to sit in the back. "If you sit in the front," the professor would tell the students, "I won't have to talk so loudly." But still they sat in the back.

Someone finally hit on an idea—it was adopted and the problem was solved. The solution? The first five rows of seats were upholstered; the remaining rows were left with hardwood seats. After that, almost everyone tried to get to class early so they could sit down front.

The Case of Nothing Like Attention and a Kind Word

Here's another success story, engineered by a Midwestern florist who noticed that many hospital nurses frequently went without recognition of any kind for their efforts, whether perceived as helpful or not. Whenever he sent flowers to a hospital patient, he always enclosed a single, separate carnation with a card saying, "For your favorite nurse."

Nurses who received them (including the men) pinned them on their uniforms, and in the cafeteria there was always conversation about "Whose favorite nurse are you?"

As one of the nurses explained, "Usually, the only way for a patient to express gratitude is with a 'Thank you' at the end of a stay. This way, everybody was a winner. Nurses got recognition. The patient was still around to receive more of the TLC. And it didn't hurt the florist's business, either."

The Case of Pick It Up!

Meanwhile, nearer home, you have undoubtedly heard your neighbor complain that her daughter simply will not pick up after herself, no matter how often she is told. If you were to listen to a conversation between this parent and someone skilled in the use of our checklist, you might hear:

"She doesn't pick up after herself, even though you've made it clear you expect her to?"

"I've told her and I've told her, but it doesn't do any good."

"And she knows where to put the clothes?"

"Of *course* she does. She isn't stupid, you know."

"Sorry. Ah, tell me—what is the result of her not picking up after herself?"

"The result? The result is that I spend half *my* time picking up after her. *That's* the result!"

"I understand. But what's the result to *her*?"

"I nag."

"And how about if she does pick up?"

"What do you mean?"

"Does something favorable happen if she picks up after herself for a certain period of time—like an extra movie, or a round of applause from the family, or a favorite meal, or something else she might like to have?"

"Certainly *not*! You don't think I'm going to *bribe* her to do something she oughta wanna do anyhow, do you?"

NOTE: *Bribe* is a loaded word, implying something illegal or designed to make someone do something against his or her will. But bribery is a *legal* concept, pure and simple. Bribery means to offer inducement to someone to do something illegal—fix a parking ticket, throw a race, award a contract, etc. What we're talking about is a *positive consequence* that, if you like loaded words, could as well be called a *reward.* By providing a positive consequence, you increase the probability that behavior will occur. Even when you do something you don't like to do (when, say, you submit to surgery), you do it because you expect that life will be improved as a result. But you don't look on "getting better as a result of surgery" as a bribe. When a mother says to her child, "If you pick up your clothes for a week, I'll take you to a movie," it is not bribery. It is the offer of an incentive (a consequence desired by the child) in return for performance desired by the mother. If it were *illegal* to pay people to pick up their clothing, *then* you could rightfully call it bribery. But only then.

In this case, the performance discrepancy is that the youngster doesn't pick up her clothes in the desired manner with the desired regularity. She knows how to do it, but doesn't. Thus, the discrepancy is not likely to be eliminated by training or instruction. Her world doesn't get brighter if she does as expected; and, since she's so used to being nagged that she doesn't even hear it, her world doesn't get dimmer if she doesn't. In effect, nothing meaningful happens one way or the other. In the absence of a consequence meaningful to her for performing as desired, she tends not to perform.

Again, it is easy to say that she should pick up after herself because it is the adult thing, the right thing, the moral thing, the mother-saving thing, etc. And some day, probably, she *will* pick up after herself, because it will matter to her self-concept or her convenience or her marriage to do so. But right now there are none of these *internal* consequences. If the mother expects her daughter to perform, then she must see to it that the child's performance is followed by an *external* consequence that has value for the child.

A Case of How Smooth Is It?

Another interesting example is found in the inspection department of a manufacturing company where one of the duties is to inspect incoming materials. The features to be evaluated include the smoothness of various metal surfaces. The inspector checks to see if the smoothness meets or surpasses specifications. If it does, the material is accepted and sent on to the production department. If not smooth enough, the material is returned to the vendor.

It was noticed that inspectors were rejecting material that was, in fact, smooth enough to be accepted. "We have a training problem," said a manager. "We need to teach these inspectors to be more accurate in their smoothness judgments."

To the question, "What is the consequence of performing as desired?" a double answer appeared. To the inspectors, the result of rejecting a good batch was nothing. The batch went back to the vendor; and the vendor, knowing the game, probably let it sit in the warehouse for a month or so and then resubmitted it. On the other hand, accepting a bad batch brought the wrath of the production department down on an inspector's head. Right now.

So now we have: No noticeable consequence for rejecting a good batch of material (undesirable performance); punishment for accepting a bad batch of material (also undesirable performance). The result was that the inspectors, without even realizing it, gradually rejected more and more good batches in order to avoid the punishment that came with accepting a bad one. This was not a conscious action; it just happened.

Several options might serve for correcting this kind of problem. Management could act to make both undesirable alternatives equally undesirable to the inspectors. Since the inspectors *want* to perform well, one could also make the accuracy of their performance more

immediately visible to them. If inspectors knew they were making a bad decision, they wouldn't make it. In this case, performance feedback would probably do the trick.

Actually, however, a third alternative was selected, mostly because of the awkwardness and time needed in providing immediate feedback during inspection. Since this situation combined both a need for skill maintenance and a no-consequence problem, a little device was constructed with which the inspectors could periodically check their smoothness perceptions. The device provided a number of graded-samples for inspectors to judge, and then told them whether they were right or wrong. They weren't learning anything they didn't already know, but they *were* keeping their skill sharpened. It would also have helped to equalize the consequence for either of the undesired performances (accepting a bad batch or rejecting a good one) or to have increased the consequence of good performance. But to our knowledge this was not arranged.

———————

As mentioned elsewhere, many discrepancies have elements of more than one cause; this was one such example.

Examples of "no-consequence" situations are all around us:

"The manager is not walking the store."

"The manager isn't delegating."

"Employees don't show enough courtesy to customers."

"Meat cutters aren't cutting the meat right."

In every one of these examples (from our files) the answers to the consequence questions were negative. It didn't matter whether a performance was done in the desired manner or in some other manner. Oh, it mattered to *somebody*, all right, or the problem wouldn't have become visible. But even though performance mattered a great deal in some of these cases, the mattering didn't consist of consequences that impinge on the performers themselves. Whenever you hear any of the following:

"They should do it because it's good for the company,"

"Our image will suffer if they don't _____,"

"What will the neighbors think if you don't _____?"

"All hell breaks loose here when you don't _____,"

"It's the patriotic thing to do,"

"It's the professional thing to do,"

"It's the adult thing to do,"

"It's the Christian thing to do,"

"They just don't seem to realize how their actions affect others,"

you are hearing descriptions of situations in which the consequences or results, large though they may be to someone, are probably not having any effect on those at whom the finger is being pointed.

The Case of the Delicious Duplication Caper

During a workshop on performance analysis, two pleasant women recounted an experience they described as "delicious." They began:

"Among other things, we're responsible for duplicating professors' tests by the deadlines set for the examinations. Most of the professors bring in their items in enough time for us to do the duplication without any trouble. Only one was always late."

"What happened when he was late?"

"Oh, then we had to drop everything at the last minute, and we had to be late with some of our other work. It was very exasperating."

"But what was the consequence to the professor?"

"Ahh, but *that's* the *point*. We finally figured out that we were experiencing all the consequences. So the very next time he brought his items in late, we said, 'Sorry, professor, but your items are too late to include in the test,' and went on about our business. Well, you should have seen him! Practically had a tantrum. Ranted and raved, got all flushed in the face. But you know what?"

"No. What?"

"He has *never, ever* been late since!"

Once they understood the problem (no consequences *to the professor* for undesired performance), the solution was clear. Make it matter *to the performers;* arrange consequences.

––––––––––

When hunting for consequences that follow desired and undesired performance, be sure to keep in mind that it is the consequences to the performers that matter rather than the consequences to the boss, the parent, the organization, or the economy. It is the perception of the performers that matters; how they see it is what controls the outcome.

––––––––––

The Case of the Perfectly Puzzled Lecturer

That important point was brought home to us again during a discussion with the chief neurosurgeon of a large hospital. He was describing the time he had decided to offer a series of afternoon lectures to medical aides. He wanted to help them understand the larger picture—*why* they were taking blood pressure, blood samples, and so forth—so that they might feel more a part of the treatment team. A noble mission, and yet . . . Listen to how it turned out:

"About 40 showed up for the first lecture, and every one of them seemed eager for the information. Many of them gathered around me to ask questions when the lecture was over.

"But only about half of them showed up for the second lecture. Again, they all seemed eager and asked lots of questions.

"Only half of *them*, about ten, showed up for the third lecture. As before, they all seemed eager and asked questions. But I couldn't understand why attendance was cut in half each time. So I asked the head nurse what happened to them."

"They quit!" was the reply.

"Quit? But *why?*"

"Well, when they finally realized the importance of what they were doing, they quit to avoid the heavy responsibility."

Here was an instance in which desired performance wasn't perceived as punishing until the aides learned the "why's" of their work. So never mind whether *you* perceive the consequences as rewarding or punishing—what matters is how the performer perceives it.

Finally, how often, when you have guests, do you rush over to where the kids are playing quietly in the corner and say, "Hey, kids, you're doing a *great* job of playing quietly in the corner"? Or do you, like most of us, wait until they start acting up and then rush over to scold?

One can argue that you are, at best, providing no consequence for desired behavior. There may be favorable results for playing quietly in the corner, but *you* aren't the source of them.

A gloomier view of the situation is this: If *attention from parent* is viewed by your child as desirable, what must he or she do to get it? When you ignore episodes of peace and quiet but attend to the uproars, you strengthen the likelihood that you will be confronted by an uproar. Put a bit more bluntly, you are engineering the situation to give you something you say you don't want.

An old expression fits here: It's the squeaky wheel that gets the grease. Might not this be why people feel that to get action they must do something other than behave in a manner resembling "sitting quietly in the corner"?

We're not suggesting, by the way, that you "spoil" your children by refraining from admonition when they misbehave. We are only making the point that when you forget to "glow after good" and only "growl after bad," you run the risk of making the growl a rosier consequence than you intend.

Summing Up

When you're dealing with a situation where performers seem not to be rewarded or punished for doing it right or doing it wrong, look to see whether there are any consequences at all for performing.

If such consequences do exist, check whether these consequences impinge on the performer. If not, arrange one or more consequences that *do*.

When you want someone to perform in some particular manner, the rule is: **Make it matter.**

What to Do

Determine whether there is a meaningful consequence for the desired performance.

How to Do It

Ask these questions:

- Does performing as desired lead to consequences that are felt by the performer?

- Is there a favorable outcome for performing?

- Is there an undesirable outcome for not performing?

- Is there a source of satisfaction for performing?

- Can the person take pride in this performance as an individual or as a member of a group?

- Is there satisfaction of personal needs from performing as desired?

Part IV
Are There Other Causes?

Could They Do It if They Really Had To?

Needless to say, if people already know how to perform as expected, but aren't performing that way, the solutions you've been collecting will probably make the discrepancy go away.

But if they don't know how to do what they're expected to do, then you need to find out whether or not you'll need to turn to what is usually a more expensive solution, that of training. That's what we'll sort out now.

7

Is It a Skill Deficiency?

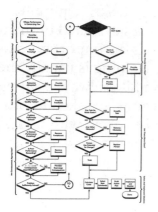

WHERE WE ARE

*A performance discrepancy exists,
and we have located several possible
remedies. The search goes on.
We need to know whether the
discrepancy exists because of a skill
deficiency—because the performers
don't know <u>how</u> to do what's
expected of them.*

Having found clues to the cause(s) of the discrepancy in the most obvious places, it's time to dig a little deeper. So in this step we explore to determine whether the performance discrepancy is due to a *skill deficiency*. In essence, are non-performers not performing as desired because they *don't know how* to do it? If their lives depended on it, would they *still* not be able to perform?

If a genuine lack of skill is not the problem, then you can forget training as a potential solution. After all, "teaching" people what they already know how to do isn't going to affect the performance discrepancy. When people already know how to do something but don't do it, then the solutions lie elsewhere. On the other hand, when a genuine skill deficiency exists, then something has to be "fixed." You will either need to change an existing skill level by teaching new skills or change what people are required to do. That is, you will either have to teach them what they can't do now, or find ways to simplify or change the size or nature of the task so that it is within their capability.

In actual practice, most of the time it's likely that your problem won't be caused by a genuine lack of skill. Except for performers who are new to their jobs, or the jobs are new to the performers (new processes, procedures, tasks, equipment, etc.), people usually will be able to do what's expected of them and will need little or no training. This is an important discovery that should cause you to rejoice. Training is usually the most costly, time-consuming solution, and it is always exciting to discover that the expensive solution you were asked to provide ("I've got a training problem") can be solved with far less cost and effort. *Convincing* someone that training isn't the answer is another matter.

Examples from Life

The following cases illustrate discrepancies that exist because—or not because—of skill deficiencies.

A Case of Sagging Motivation

The manager of a machine shop complained, "This machinist simply isn't motivated enough to do this job." We asked him what the machinist did that caused him to complain about motivation.

"He just takes forever to get his work done."

"Does he know what's expected of him?"

"Oh, sure. He's got detailed blueprints of every job, and we talk about the deadlines. But that doesn't seem to help. He's still slow."

To make a long story short, it turned out that this machinist was highly skilled, using his tools and machinery to turn out perfect products. And motivation wasn't his problem. He really wanted to do a good job and was rewarded by compliments from his colleagues when he did. So why couldn't he work as fast as expected—as fast as the other machinists? Math. He just wasn't good at translating the mathematical specifications on the blueprints into action. In addition, he had trouble remembering whether .0001 meant one thousandth of an inch or one ten-thousandth of an inch. And this lack of math skill slowed him down. A lot.

The solution was to provide some coaching on decimal numbers, after which he began working nearly as fast as everyone else. What started out as a "motivation" problem ended up as a lack of skill in a small, but critical, part of the job.

The Case of the Candy Caper

The manager of a medium-sized food company announced, "I've got a training problem, and I want you to develop a training program to solve it." We asked him to explain.

"In our new plant we make only six varieties of our candies; and because we have only six varieties, our sales reps travel around in panel trucks with a supply of each. In a sense, each rep is a traveling warehouse."

"And the problem?"

"The reps are pushing only *one* product instead of all six. I want you to teach them to sell all products equally."

"Do they know they're supposed to sell all six products?

"Of course. We've told them many times."

"Do they know *how* to sell the other five?"

"Of course. It's no different from the one they are pushing."

"Do they know as much about those other five as they do about the one they're selling well?"

"Certainly they do. We have a good product course, and they have been carefully trained in all of the products."

"So they could sell the others if their lives depended on it?"

"Of course. But they don't."

"Do you have any idea why they don't push those other five products?"

"Well, yes. I suppose it's because they get three times as much commission for the one as they do for the other five. But they ought to want to sell the others *anyhow*."

Aha! What started out to be one of those "I've got a training problem" episodes turned out to be something entirely different. The performance discrepancy was clearly *not* due to a lack of skill. The sales reps *could* sell the products, but they didn't. In this case, training was clearly not the remedy. What would you teach? What would you put into a course? What information could be imparted that the reps didn't already have? True, you could lecture them on the importance of selling the products equally (if they didn't already know that). Or you could explain how their jobs depend on their selling those other five products (if that were really true). But training will not make any difference in their *skill* at doing that which the manager wants them to do. Since they already knew how to do as desired, the answer was not training. It was something else.

A Case of Handwriting on the Walls

A principal complained, "We've got to teach these kids not to write on the toilet walls."

But what would you put into a course on Non-toilet-wall Writing? Can't you just see the curriculum?

Monday: Introduction to Non-Writing

Tuesday: History of Non-writing

Wednesday: Toilet Appreciation

Thursday: Famous Johns and Their Dastardly Defacement

Friday: Pot Power

A Case of It's No Accident

Managers are often heard to say, "If only we could make these people more safety conscious." One interview with a manager went like this:

"Safety is a real problem for you?"

"Yes, it is. Every year we lose two million dollars because of accidents."

"Do you think your employees can recognize a safety hazard when they see one?"

"Oh, sure. Most of them have been around for some time, and they know what's safe and what isn't."

"Do they know how to report a safety hazard?"

"Yes, but they don't. And they oughta wanna do more about safety. It's in their own best interest. We need to teach them to be more safety conscious."

So the manager put safety posters on the walls and insisted that employees watch safety films on a regular basis.

Nothing much happened to the accident rate, as might be expected, for this was another of those cases where people knew how to perform as desired, but didn't. An important performance discrepancy existed, but it was *not due* to a skill deficiency. In such cases the question is not what to teach, but rather how to rearrange things to get the performance that is already available.

Whenever you hear someone say, "They oughta wanna," or some variation thereof (usually accompanied by the waggling of a forefinger), it is almost certain that you are *not* dealing with a skill deficiency. It is almost certain that the people *could* perform as desired if the conditions and the consequences were right.

- The sales reps know how to sell the products, but they don't; they *oughta wanna.*
- Kids *oughta wanna* brush their teeth without being nagged by their parents.
- The legal staff *oughta wanna* settle more cases out of court.

No amount of information, no amount of exhortation, is necessarily going to change an "oughta wanna" situation. What's needed is a change in the conditions or the consequences surrounding the desired performance. "You oughta wanna do it *for your own good*" is not a potent motivator; it is one of the weakest techniques known for influencing anyone to do something he or she already knows how to do.

Loose Language

In thinking about this issue, we wonder if the trouble doesn't spring from the imprecision with which many people so often use our language. They say things like, "I'll *teach* you to sass your mother." But this does not mean that the speaker intends to instruct the sasser in how to sass the sassee. It means that the speaker intends, through the arrangement of conditions and consequences (whap!), to modify the performance of the sasser—to cause that child to do something he or she already knows how to do; namely, to refrain from sassing.

Perhaps this explains the genesis of the expression, "I've got a training problem." It seems that often when a difference is perceived between what someone is doing and what others would like that person to be doing, they conclude that the way to reduce the difference is by training, by instruction. But training is only one of the remedies for a performance discrepancy. In fact, training is only one of the remedies *even when* a genuine skill deficiency exists.

After all, there are different "forms" of skill deficiencies. Sometimes people can't do it today because they have *forgotten* how, and sometimes because they *never knew* how. Solutions for these situations are different. And sometimes people don't do the job because they can't—perhaps they lack the mental capacity or the physical strength. Again, a different solution is called for.

Sometimes you may find it hard to judge whether a skill deficiency is involved, or how much of a deficiency it is. If records don't tell you whether the skill was once present, and you can't tell by watching people as they try to do the thing they are suspected of not doing, then you might try the direct approach. Talk to some of them and ask them whether *they* feel their skill is weak or whether something else is causing the discrepancy.

Summing Up

When you detect an important performance discrepancy, do not automatically assume that it is a "training problem" and that the solution involves teaching/training, even when you are dealing with a skill deficiency. Before taking action, determine whether the performance discrepancy is due to a genuine skill deficiency.

What to Do

Determine whether the discrepancy is due to a genuine skill deficiency.

How to Do It

Ask these questions:

- Could the person do it if really required to do it?
- Could the person do it if his or her life depended on it?
- Are the person's present skills adequate for the desired performance?

If it makes sense, ask the person who's not performing:

- What might you learn how to do that would make your job easier?

8

Could They Do It in the Past?

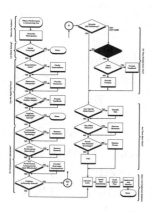

WHERE WE ARE

A performance discrepancy exists and is considered important. It has been established that it is a genuine skill deficiency. They couldn't do it if their lives depended on it.

Shucks," said the elderly gentleman, "I used to know how to do that pretty good. You just give me a day or two to practice getting the kinks out, and I'll be right in there with the best of 'em."

If he's right, what a waste it would be to start teaching him the skill from the very beginning. In terms of what has to be done to get rid of a skill deficiency, there's a great difference between the skill that *used to be* and the skill that *never was.* Yet the number of instances in which we make the mistake of trying to teach people something they already know is very large indeed.

So once you've established that you are dealing with a genuine skill deficiency, the thing to do next is ask: Could they do it in the past? If they could, they should require far less training to get them back up to speed than if they never knew how to perform in the first place.

Determining whether a lack of skill is due to a form of forgetting or to a lack of training is one of the more important decisions in the analysis of performance discrepancies. It's also one of the more neglected decisions.

> **NOTE:** Even when it's plain that a genuine skill deficiency exists and that a person has *never had* the skill, the solution is not necessarily a formal training program. This issue is explored in a coming chapter, but it isn't too early for a cautionary note: *Beware of concluding that a genuine skill deficiency exists.* It's amazing how many courses are given under the assumption that students know nothing whatsoever about the main topic until taught otherwise. All of the students are made to wade through all of the material from the beginning. This can waste a lot of time and may create misconceptions about the effectiveness of a course where the teacher succeeds in "teaching" what the students already knew.

If you have ever gotten involved with children and ended up cricking your back while playing games or bending your ego as you floundered over eighth-grade mathematics, you will agree that time can play havoc with skills that used to exist. It happens in jobs, too. Consider the following example:

The Case of the Reviled Radar Tech

Several years ago, one of us was a member of a team assigned to assess the proficiency of radar technicians who had graduated from a military course designed to teach that occupational specialty. The team traveled to locations around the country to test each technician on his own equipment. While the radar tech waited outside, the team "inserted a trouble" into the radar equipment. The tech was then shown one symptom, much as happens when a radar operator discovers that something isn't working.

One young man tested did an incredibly poor job, even though he had done well during his training that ended some months previously. He hardly knew where things were located, let alone what to do to find the troubles. Here, it seemed, was a performance discrepancy of large proportions. When the results of the test were reported, as was required, his commanding officer exploded.

"Get that man in here," he roared. "I'll teach *him* to make our unit look bad."

Fortunately, he was persuaded to sit still long enough to answer a few questions.

"How long has this man been assigned to your unit?" he was asked.

"About six months."

"What has he been doing during that time?"

"He's been assigned as an oiler."

"How much time has he spent inside the radar van?"

"Well, none. I just told you he's been assigned as an oiler."

"So he hasn't had any practice or experience in radar maintenance since he joined your outfit?"

". . . No, I guess not."

Here, then, was a technician who had spent several months learning a rather complex skill; but for the following six months had had no opportunity to practice that skill. No wonder his test performance was poor. No wonder there was a difference between what he could do and what he was expected to be able to do.

The battery commander also saw the point. Instead of chastising the man, he assigned him immediately to maintenance duty (under the watchful eye of a more experienced man).

This was an instance in which:

- There was a genuine performance discrepancy.
- It was important to remedy.
- It was due to a skill deficiency.
- The skill was once there but had been forgotten.

It was a classic case of a skill withering away for lack of exercise. Other examples are not hard to find.

Some capabilities fade with age. On a physical level, it's unlikely that you can still suck your big toe. But it's conceivable that although you can still throw a ball, you can't throw it as hard and straight as you once did. Can you do the splits, or dash a speedy 100 meters? Or, if we look at mental tasks, how about naming the gods in Vulcan mythology, reciting Hamlet's soliloquy, proving Pythagorean's theorem, diagramming a sentence, using a slide rule? Well, you get the point. Skills you once had fade away unless kept alive by practice. But if they are not completely dead, they may be revived with something much smaller than a formal course.

A Case a Little Closer to Home

Getting a little personal now . . .

RFM: Peter, didn't you used to live in San Francisco?

PP: Yes.

RFM: Then how come you get lost when you drive there?

PP: Come on, now. I don't always get lost. Just most of the time.

RFM: Why?

PP: Well, it all seems so familiar that I don't bother with maps—and then I find I've forgotten some of the streets. I don't get much practice any more. Haven't you ever forgotten anything from lack of practice?

RFM: Not very much. Only most of what I learned in school.
PP: Wastrel!
RFM: Wait a minute! I remember from seventh-grade biol-
         ogy that the esophagus has a pyloric valve on the end
         of it.
PP: How nice. What else do you remember?
RFM: Ah-h . . . mmm . . . well. . .
PP: Didn't you used to be good at math?
RFM: Not actually good, but I used to know how to solve
         calculus problems and how to do things like analysis
         of variance. But I couldn't do them today. Never
         needed to after I left graduate school.
PP: But you could relearn them, don't you think?
RFM: Sure I could. And in less time than it took the first time
         around.
PP: Exactly the point. You used to be able to do things you
         can't do now, but you could relearn them in less time
         than it took first time around.

In none of these cases would we propose the expensive route
of formal courses of instruction. If we want to sustain these
once-known skills at an acceptable level, then the need is probably for a "skill maintenance program" of the kind described in
the next chapter.

Summing Up

In this chapter we've called your attention to the importance of those questions that help you decide whether a skill deficiency is due to some form of forgetting or to the fact that it never existed. If it never existed, there's a good chance that training will be indicated. But if it once existed and now is lost, strayed, or stolen, training from scratch would be a more expensive remedy than you need. More likely, practice and feedback will be all that is needed.

Whether you answer "yes" or "no" to "Could they do it in the past?" (Did each person once know how to perform as desired?), there's another question to answer before you will know what remedies to suggest or select. We'll consider that question next.

What to Do

Determine whether the skill once existed.

How to Do It

Ask these questions:

• Did the person once know how to perform as desired?

• Has the person forgotten how to do what needs to be done?

9

Is the Skill Used Often?

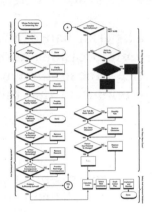

WHERE WE ARE

An important performance discrepancy exists, and it is a genuine skill deficiency. We have discovered that at one time the person was able to perform as desired.

It is not uncommon for people to discover that, even though they once knew how to do something well, they've either lost their "edge" or lost entirely the ability to do what once they did with ease. When a skill fades or disappears, an appropriate remedy to consider is a skill maintenance program. Skill maintenance programs come in two major forms.

Periodic Practice

One kind is meant to help someone "stay in practice." It is a systematic honing of an important skill or state of knowledge that has to be used only occasionally. The police departments of the country recognized long ago that though police officers rarely use their weapons, they must be able to do so quickly and accurately when the need arises. To keep their accuracy at an acceptable level, officers are required to practice regularly on a pistol range—an example of a performance maintenance program.

The concert pianist practices and practices between concerts, not only to increase his or her skill, but to maintain it. Pianists know that the fine edge of an existing skill can deteriorate rather quickly.

Both of these examples are cases in which performance (and peak performance, at that) is required only occasionally or infrequently. In these cases, periodic practice is the useful remedy. The more critical the skill, the more important that this practice be provided.

Practice with Feedback

The second kind of skill maintenance program—practice with feedback—is needed in a different situation. This is the case where:

- A skill deficiency exists.
- The person used to be able to perform the skill well.
- *The skill is in constant use.*

These are situations in which, paradoxically, performance deteriorates *despite* constant practice. And this is a totally different problem from situations where performance withered away because of *lack* of practice.

But isn't it true that "practice makes perfect"?

Unfortunately, that ragged old adage is misleading. Practice makes perfect *only* when you have information about how well you are practicing. In fact, if you have no way of knowing how well you are doing, practice may serve merely to entrench poor or imperfect actions. Your marksmanship will not be improved if you merely shoot at the moon. Your pronunciation of a foreign language will not improve unless you can hear the difference between your way of speaking and a native's way of speaking. Practice without feedback is of little value.

The Case of the Slipping Solderers

In an electronics assembly plant, high precision was demanded of women soldering components together. On joining the company, they were taught to solder, and they were not allowed on the production line until they could consistently make acceptable solder joints. On the job, it was found that the quality of soldered joints tended to fall off after a few weeks, even though the women made hundreds of joints each day. Why?

It was hard to get feedback about the quality of each soldered joint as it was made. You couldn't necessarily tell just by looking. It wasn't practical to make immediate mechanical and electrical tests of each connection. Faulty work in a subassembly may not have been discovered until many joints had been made by many operators. Tracking down the faulty connection and the operator concerned was possible, but costly.

Once again, a performance maintenance program was useful. This time, though, practice was not the primary need, because the soldering task was "practiced" hundreds of times a day. Here it *maintained* skill level by providing the operator with periodic feedback about the quality of her work. All operators were required to renew their certificate of competence every six months. If they checked out, fine; if not, they were given some brief brush-up training. This, it was found, was enough to keep them up to snuff.

The Case of the Diminishing Driver

A friend complained, "That's the *third* traffic ticket I've had in a month. I've been driving for ten years and never had a citation—and all of a sudden they start picking on me!"

Hmmm. Wasn't it more likely that his driving skill had slipped somewhat, even though he got plenty of practice? After all, you don't find out about (get feedback for) every infraction, for every display of poor or dangerous car handling. There is no one there to inform you each time you forget to use a turn signal, or cut another driver short, or make a turn from the wrong lane, or follow another car too closely. When people do get feedback in the form of a traffic citation, they seldom recognize this as an indication of slipshod driving; instead, there is the tendency to point that ever-ready finger— in someone else's direction. (If fingers were as lethal as 45s, we'd all be dead by now.)

The Case of the Perpetual Performers

"But I interview more than a dozen people a day," grumped the manager, "and now you tell me I don't do it right? I get more practice at interviewing than anyone in the plant."

She was right. She interviewed more people than anyone else around. And yet . . . and yet there was something about her performance that rubbed people the wrong way. Here was still another instance in which the performance was less than adequate, even though the skill was exercised frequently.

What was happening? No feedback. She never found out that she was irritating some of her interviewees. The people interviewed certainly wouldn't tell her, and those who heard them grumble only commented among themselves. So why should this manager behave differently when there was no feedback to suggest that the performance was less than satisfactory?

It Happens All the Time

Isn't this something we all experience in everyday living? We spend a lot of time interacting with others, and hence get a lot of practice at it. Yet how often does someone take us aside and offer real honest-to-goodness feedback that would help us do it better? Practically never, right? When was the last time you got feedback on your table manners? Or on our business etiquette? How often do you wonder about whether you said "the wrong thing" because everyone is too polite to tell you?

Summing Up

Any time performance is something other than what is desired, and there is reason to believe that the desired performance could be within the person's capabilities, check to see whether he or she is receiving regular information about the quality of the performance.

If a *frequently* used skill slips, look for lack of feedback as the probable cause. If an *infrequently* used skill slips, look for lack of practice as a probable cause. Perhaps it would help to see the situation graphically.

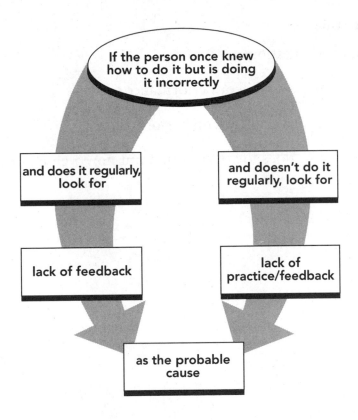

What to Do

Determine whether the lost or deteriorated skill is used frequently or infrequently.

- If the skill is used **frequently** but has deteriorated despite regular use, maintain the level of performance by providing periodic feedback.

- If the skill is used **infrequently**, maintain the level of performance by providing a regular schedule of practice with feedback.

How to Do It

Ask these questions:

- How often is the skill or performance used?

- Is there regular feedback on performance?

- Exactly how does the person find out how well he or she is doing?

10
Can the Task Be Simplified?

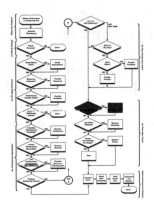

WHERE WE ARE

A genuine performance discrepancy exists, and we have determined that it is a genuine skill deficiency. In the job as currently defined, there is something the person cannot do. Before concluding that formal training is needed, we should give some thought to whether the task itself might be simplified.

We are still only exploring possibilities. By now, you may have several ideas on how to close the gap between the desired performance and what is now being done. And any of those ideas may be enough to solve all or part of the problem. In forming those ideas, however, we have assumed that the job must be done in its existing form. Nothing wrong with that if our final solution(s) are easy to put in place. But it's always worthwhile—and particularly if the solution calls for significant time and effort—to see if the job itself can be modified so that the person performing will be more likely to succeed. In other words, can we change the skill requirements to more closely fit the current capabilities of the performer(s)?

Changing the Skill Requirement

Changing the requirements of the job is often much simpler and less expensive than almost any other solution. Those who don't have the skill to perform the job as presently defined can become more productive when the job can be changed to fit their capabilities. Four ways of changing the skill requirements include:

1. Changing the criteria of successful performance.

    Do the present standards for the job call for a higher level of perfection than is really needed? If the standards for accuracy, speed, completeness, neatness, and the like were eased off a little, would it really make an unacceptable difference?

2. Helping with mental tasks.

    Instead of requiring someone to memorize lists and sequences, particularly when the information is not used often, could you substitute an "aid to recall"—a list pinned on the wall, a checklist of the sequence of steps to be performed? Could you do away with the need to remember by simply controlling the order in which materials or information arrive? Could you control the flow of work with something like the single-queue, first-come/first-served system widely used in banks and post offices?

3. Helping with physical tasks.

   Could you provide a machine for lifting heavy loads? Redesign a tool that's hard to use? (That's how Phillips head screwdrivers came to be invented.) Is it possible to rearrange the workplace, lessening the distance that has to be reached, or re-orienting a computer screen so that it doesn't put a crick in a neck?

4. Redesigning the job itself.

   Would it be possible to allocate some part of the job to another person? Maybe you could reshuffle duties so that fewer different tasks or different combinations of tasks have to be handled by each person concerned?

Some of this probably sounds obvious, particularly since we used similar thinking back in Chapter 3, "Can We Apply Fast Fixes?" In practice, the need and place for some of these changes may be less obvious—which may explain why these problems have persisted in the first place! Practices in the workplace, be it shop floor, office, or anywhere else, get nailed in place for all sorts of reasons, making it sound as if there's one, and only one, way of doing things. Those reasons include:

- Time-hallowed precedent.
  "That's the way we've always done it."

- Myths about what's accepted in high places.
  "That's what the boss wants."

- Physical or mental elitism which sorts the tough from the softies, the intellectuals from the ignorant.
  "I don't need a back support to lift heavy weights."
  "If you knew chemistry, you'd see why X comes before Y."

Now we're not saying that any of those "reasons" are necessarily wrong. But "the way we've always done it" can survive as part of the corporate mythology even in the face of serious efforts to make a change. "What the boss wants" may have been an off-hand, misunderstood remark, filtered down through the levels until it became a mythical policy statement (e.g., "Policy won't let us put authors' and contributors' names on reports."). The strong-backed elitist may not just be a blowhard giving bad advice (he lifts his body weight at the gym every evening and has the body to prove it), and the walking fount of knowledge could be right (she does "know the chemistry" and can explain why Y before X is wrong). But making others like that could still be unnecessary. So any time you bump into such a statement, test it out. Simplifying the required performance is usually better than teaching someone to do the more complicated version of the task.

Let's look at some examples under each of the four major headings. As you read, see if you can think of a parallel example from the problems you have to deal with.

Changing the Criteria

No matter how the present standards of competent performance came into being, look at each of them and ask: "Why do we have this standard? Are we demanding more than we need in terms of rate of working, accuracy, finish, completeness, etc.?"

The first, rate of working, is always worth probing. Unacceptable errors can creep into the picture whenever someone must keep on rushing to deliver according to an arbitrary definition of "on time." You know the old question: "Why not get it right the first time, rather than taking time to fix it later?" What does it cost to repair those "Hurry up" mistakes?

Several other questions may help change your viewpoint about the way job and/or task criteria are currently defined.

Change the questions as needed to fit the task you're looking at:

Do we really need to finish this surface to one-ten-thousandth of an inch?

Is it true that the colors or pattern must match precisely?

Does the layout of the letter have to exactly match the style book?

Will it matter if the cherry is off-center on the whipped cream?

Can we accept a few daisies in the lawn or must it be daisy-free?

Do these videotapes really have to conform to network production standards?

A word of warning: It may take both courage and diplomacy to start probing issues of this sort.

Helping with Mental Tasks

Examples abound where "know-how" is needed, but where nobody would think of providing a training course as a solution. That notoriously difficult task of programming a VCR—assuming you don't have a young teenager on hand—should be handled by looking at the instruction book. Bought a new car and unsure of how to work the windshield washer or set the radio buttons? Just read the manual. It's simpler than a course.

Even in a case where "doing it right, no errors" is critical because nasty consequences follow incorrect performance, a similar solution works well. Using a fire extinguisher, for example, requires a small but critical amount of knowledge. Rather than try to store information in everybody's head by presenting a course on fire fighting, you put instructions where they can be seen, right on the side of each extinguisher.

If you need an extinguisher in a hurry but have forgotten how to use it, it takes only a second or two to refresh your memory.

In the best of all possible worlds, every household might have available at all times a person able to render first aid for all conceivable cases of poisoning. Even now, most of us take care of that problem adequately by fastening a list of poison antidotes to the door of the broom closet. (And maybe some do the on-line equivalent by hitting computer keys to summon the information onto their screens.) Whatever the method, storing accurate information where it's readily available may be preferable to trying to remember what to do in the panic of an emergency.

The captain of a jetliner, no matter how grizzled and wise, must use a checklist to ensure that all items are checked during the pre-flight inspection. There's nothing unprofessional about using such an aid; in fact, the unprofessional is the one who tries to get away without using the memory aid.

And imagine the chaos if every person who prepared airline tickets had to remember all the information there is to know about fares, flight times, destinations, flight numbers, days the flights are operative, and a gaggle of other details. Even if such were possible, the problem would be multiplied every time there was a *change* in ticket prices and schedules. With the information stored in a computer instead of stuffed into someone's head, it is easily and accurately available and easy to change.

Prompting works even when it's not as complete as a manual or checklist. In fact, "shorthand" is desirable in some cases: "In an emergency, dial 911." Or even "Emergency 911." Labels on controls help prevent errors by the new or infrequent user.

Snappy rules and acronyms work well, too: Which way to screw the canister onto a gas mask? "Righty-tighty, lefty-loosey." The "rule of the road" when passing the colored buoys which mark the channel as you sail your yacht in and out of harbor is: "Red right returning." And everyone remembers: "i before e, except after c." (That's the rule, as someone noted, that raises spelling to a sceince.)

The Case of the Meter Readers

Consider the case of the meter readers. Women at the end of a production line making electronic products recorded the electrical characteristics of each product so that an accept/reject decision could be made. To do so, they took about six readings from as many meters, and wrote down the numbers on a card.

In an ordinary day, each woman made hundreds of readings; and many of them had had months, even years, of experience. But when their meter-reading accuracy was measured one day, it was found to be only 40 percent! Interestingly, a group of women with no special training in reading meters performed at the same level. But when the analog meters (with pointers showing the readings along one or another scale) were replaced by digital meters that displayed the readings in numbers, performance instantly shot up to near perfect accuracy. The meter-reading task was made considerably easier simply by eliminating the need for careful interpretation of often difficult-to-read scales.

Color Coding

Aids to performance don't have to be in words, even. A useful way of helping people "distinguish one from another," widely used because it lessens the need for remembering, is color-coding. Color-coded pathways on the floor tell forklift operators where to travel and where to store items in a warehouse, or guide patients to hospital departments, or travelers to trains. Color-coding indicates what gas is stored in a cylinder; colored bands tell the value of the resistors used in electrical circuits; at the gas station, color on the pumps tells octane ratings. Colored price tags in clothing stores are often coded to indicate size or to denote sale items.

A note of caution: Color-coding is not always well used. Picture one of us in the control room of an anonymous nuclear power plant. On one side of the room is a twelve-foot shelf filled with large red binders.

Us: What are those binders for?

Them: Oh, they're guides for procedures we have to follow.

Us: Any reason they're colored red?

Them: Yes, those are emergency procedures.

Us: Covering all sorts of emergencies?

Them: Yes. We have to refer to them and "do it by the book" any time we have an emergency.

Us: Since they all look alike, how do you know which binder to use for a particular emergency?

Them: Well . . . uh . . . you . . . just know.

Shapes

Using different shapes is another useful aid in sorting "this one" from "that one." The control that puts the wheels down in an aircraft has a round end, the one that works the flaps has a square end. You can tell by feel which handle is which, without distraction from the important task of looking where you're going. On an assembly line, the hole or socket into which a part is fitted has a distinctive shape (square pegs and round holes, remember) so that nothing goes together unless you have the right part, properly aligned. The three prongs on the end of your power cords make it impossible to plug them in upside down.

The Case of the Careless Copier

Take this example we ran into at a large company that makes copying machines. People in the marketing department had noted that an unusually large number of customers were having difficulties with one model of copier.

"They just don't know how to insert the toner bottle." (That's a plastic bottle filled with the black powder that makes the printed image.) "All they have to do is slide it along IN the track, but they slide it ON TOP of the track instead. That creates a mess as the toner spews all over the machine, and the customer calls the maintenance people. It's damned expensive."

As you might expect, the first solution proposed was to train the customers. Analysis showed, however, that the performance discrepancy was a "sort-of" skill deficiency; the operators could sort-of do it if they really had to, but they found it hard to do it correctly without paying a great deal of attention. The solution? Further analysis revealed that the task could be simplified by painting a red stripe on the machine where the toner bottle was to be inserted, and a similar stripe on the bottles themselves. The instruction could then be simply, "Line up the stripes when inserting the bottle." The cost of this proposed solution was about $15,000. Compared to what it might have cost to train customers to perform the task more accurately without the performance aid, it was a good solution, indeed.

Helping with Physical Tasks

This is the "ergonomic" area, making the job easier to handle by changing the environment in some way.

When heavy objects have to be lifted, plainly you need a performance aid such as a crane or forklift. Less obvious is the case where a not-so-heavy object has to be lifted many times, in which effort is exerted over time. In such a case, performance may improve if the height or distance of lifting can be reduced, or conveyor rollers provided. In the office, poor performance on the word processor is often attributed to carpal tunnel syndrome, which, in turn, is often tied to poor positioning of hands and keyboard—a sort of domino effect. Changing something earlier in the chain (the hand position) eases the strain, which eases the damage to the wrist, leading to better typing.

Other ways in which work can be simplified include providing better access to what has to be done. Improving visual or physical access to the task—making it easier to see or get to the things that need doing—and clarifying the information to be used are examples. Plumbers, for example, find it much easier to install food disposers under a sink before all the carpentry work encloses the space. Electricians find it much easier to get to the places where they need to string wire before the open spaces are covered by the wallboard.

Redesigning the Job

The most obvious example is to allocate some part of the job to someone else. If the pace of work is such as to invite mistakes, or if the attention of the performer has to be directed in several directions at the same time, or if doing it right takes three hands, consider splitting off some part of the operation.

If there's great variability in the job, with each variation calling for different skills, maybe you should split the job, making each person a specialist and limiting the range of problems to be dealt with by each. Perhaps part of one performer's job can be swapped for another's?

Finally, performance can often be improved simply by allowing workers to periodically swap jobs—"You do my job for awhile and I'll do yours." Where job swapping is feasible, it helps reduce the boredom of repetitive tasks and increases worker ability to pay attention to key aspects of their work.

Summing Up

Even when a genuine skill deficiency exists, any solution to the problem should be weighed against the possibility of changing some aspect of the job, thereby overcoming the effect of the skill deficiency, at least in part.

Opportunities to incorporate one or more kinds of performance aid (checklists, instruction sheets, signs, labels, color-coding, and the like) can almost always be found.

If training seems to be the only remedy, on-the-job training may be easier and cheaper, and just as good as the formal variety. As one of the sages of the business, Thomas Gilbert, put it, "Show-how is cheaper than know-how."

What to Do

See if you can find a solution simpler than performance maintenance or formal training. Try to reduce the difficulty of the job.

How to Do It

Ask these questions:

- Can I reduce the standards by which performance is judged, particularly the "Hurry Up" demands?

- Can I change the job by providing some kind of performance aid? Can I store the needed information in a more reliable and permanent way (in written instructions, checklists, etc.) than in someone's head?

- Can I provide help with the physical demands of the job, including redesign of the workplace to allow for more efficient work?

- Can I reduce the pressure by parceling off part of this job to someone else? Or arrange for workers to swap jobs for specific periods of time?

11

Any Obstacles Remaining?

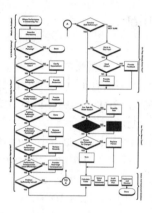

WHERE WE ARE

Before we finish sleuthing for clues and begin deciding on solution(s), we want to know whether we've missed anything. In particular, we want to know whether there may be some remaining obstacles that are a little less obvious than those we discovered in Chapter 3.

In Chapter 3, "Can We Apply Fast Fixes?", we encouraged you to look for three kinds of "sore thumb" problems, namely (1) invisible expectations which left workers in the dark about what was required of them, (2) physical obstacles that made performance unnecessarily difficult, and (3) inadequate feedback that starved people for information by which to improve what they were doing. Then in Chapter 10, "Can the Task Be Simplified?", we suggested that instead of "changing the worker," you should consider whether it might be better to "change the job."

Here the emphasis will be a little different. With likely causes and remedies in mind, you should make one last check to ensure you haven't been lured off course by any unrecognized assumptions, biases or myths—or by obstacles that may be somewhat less visible than those considered in Chapter 3.

First, we'll give you examples of how conflicts, arising from the job itself or from dealing with people, can confuse the issues. After that, we'll offer more examples of problems that can arise when standing too close to a problem.

Conflicting Demands from the Job

Let's begin with this business of conflicts.

The Ever-Ringing Telephone

Have you ever said to yourself, "I could do this job perfectly well if only the !?#$%# telephone would stop ringing so that I could concentrate for five minutes at a time!"

That's a perfect example of a situation in which a job would get done more efficiently if the conditions were changed (without, please note, the need for instruction). It's a typical problem; the victim is capable of doing what has to be done and would do an acceptable job if only he or she could get at it. You can easily identify obstacles of this kind by the direct approach; ask the performer to tell you what gets in the way of performing.

We know that in industry it is courting inefficiency, if not disaster, to organize in a way that gives a person more than one boss. Inevitably it happens that in trying to please one, he or she must neglect the interests of others. Though multiple-bossism is recognized as poor management practice, that doesn't keep it from happening, as when two or more people are required to "share" a secretary.

The Non-Teaching Teachers

Consider our schools. Politicians, the public in general, and parents in particular grumble about schools. Teachers, they say, should get in there and teach. Yet all too often teachers find themselves swamped in non-teaching activities—collecting milk money, keeping interminable records, and otherwise burning up time on chores just as well handled at a clerical level. College teachers, expected to use visual materials and computers freely, complain that the materials and help they need are available only from a remote (but oh-so-central) location, hedged about by a flurry of paperwork administered by an office that is not always open when the teacher can go there.

Apply this to your own experience: How often have you been dismayed at the way something takes a lot longer than it should because of paperwork, or the number of approvals required, all apparently justified as "the way it's done here"? Or because some functionary is "responsible for" the equipment and therefore resists tooth and nail letting the intended users use it?

Multiple Agendas

We've referred elsewhere to the problem of "multiple bossism." It's not a new problem—it's right there in the Good Book: "No man can serve two masters." No worker should be put in a position of being told on the one hand, "Do this," and on the other, "Do that." That, plainly, is bad management.

But this obstacle to good performance can be sneaky; the problem can exist even without having two people involved. For instance: Policy says one thing but what's rewarded is another (talking safety but rewarding production is the classic example). It also happens when you have a single individual who says one thing one day and something else the next.

The Case of the Multiple Assignments

Back to schools again. Typically, students have as many "bosses" as they have teachers. Each "boss" demands time and attention from the students, and often each imposes different rules. As a result, three lots of homework all have to be done the same night when they could easily have been spaced out through the week. But the students who fail to deliver all the assignments when due find themselves with unfavorable consequences. They may end up saying, "I hate school." That's not what schools say they are about, and it is an outcome that can be avoided. This is not to say that students don't goof off. But it does indicate that we might get more from students (and who might get more satisfaction from school) if we paid more attention to the conditions under which they are expected to perform.

Even worse than the problems of voices that do not sing in harmony is the problem of the "secret agenda." It takes many forms.

The Case of the Hidden Hatchet

A large company took a look at its course for management trainees. When the course was analyzed for effectiveness, it was noted that some trainees were let go at the end of instruction even though their technical performance was good or adequate. When we asked why, we were told it was because these trainees manifested some personal characteristics considered inappropriate for an executive.

Had these characteristics ever been brought to the attention of the trainees so that they might have a chance to change them? No. Why not? Because it is hard to tell a man that you don't like the color of his ties, or a woman that her blue jeans are offensive. It is easier to tell people that they are not suitable for the job, or to mumble something about performance, and drop the hatchet.

The course now includes a "personality" checklist that the training supervisor must fill out and show the trainees each month. In this way, trainees who exhibit behaviors considered objectionable by management will have an opportunity to change if they so desire.

The Case of the Elusive Evaluation

The faculty of a medical school once complained, "These students of ours will argue for hours over half a point on our *written* exams. Yet it isn't the written exams that are important. We've got to teach them to be less concerned with those darned paper-and-pencil tests." The rest of the conversation went like this:

"Do students really care about their performance on the written tests?"

"Yes. And they shouldn't. It's the *subjective* evaluations the staff makes of the students that are important."

"When is this evaluation made?"

"All day and every day our staff members are noting and evaluating each student's actual performance. We note how he or she performs with patients in the clinic, with other students, and with staff, as well as noting performance in the lab."

"How do you consolidate the results of these subjective evaluations?"

"We compare notes."

"Who does?"

"The staff. We get together and discuss the progress of each student."

"Is the student present?"

"Certainly not!"

"So the results of the *written* exams are *visible* to students, but the results of *subjective* evaluations are *in*visible to them?"

"Yes. But visible or not, it's the subjective evaluations that are really important; and that's what students really ought to be interested in."

You can imagine how difficult it was to refrain from asking point-blank, "If they're *that* important, why keep them such a big secret?"

The Case of the Masticating Menace

We met a man highly competent and creative in his field who, we were told, was avoided by friends and business associates alike. Associates dreaded having to take him along to meet clients if a meal was involved, because he chomped his food with his mouth open—and talked while doing so. He had done it for years, and for years people avoided taking him to business meals. Nobody had the nerve—or the consideration—to tell him about it.

So why should he change? *Would* he change if aware of the hidden agenda?

How many executives have been fired, kicked upstairs, or retired because their superiors had the authority but not the guts to tell them about an offensive but easy-to-correct habit?

How many teachers must there be who return test results to students days, even weeks, after the test was taken (too late for the feedback to serve much purpose), and who then complain that student performance isn't any better than it is—and that the students don't seem to care?

Might your relations with others improve if you could know how they really feel about your present words and actions? Would you be willing to give up using a particular expression, or a gesture, if you knew it was offensive to someone you cared about?

The Case of the Unappreciated Frankness

Closely related to not knowing that you are expected to do something is not knowing *when* you are expected to do it. For example, a physical scientist working in the laboratory of a rather large corporation confided that he had been rated down by his manager because of what the manager referred to as an "undesirable characteristic." The conversation went like this:

"My boss said I didn't know how to keep my mouth shut."

"And can you?"

"Of *course* I can. Discretion is the name of the game in the lab I work in. If I couldn't keep my mouth shut, I'd have been out of a job long ago."

"Then what do you suppose your manager is complaining about?"

"Well, every once in a while he calls me into a meeting and asks me to tell them what I *really* think about something or other. And I do."

"And that's bad?"

"Only sometimes. Occasionally there is someone sitting in the meeting from another division, or even from a customer's company, and I'm not aware of it. *Then* when my manager asks what I really think, he seems to want me to say something to make the company look good rather than to tell him what I really think. Trouble is . . . I can never tell when to do which."

Thus, if a person is unable to tell *when* to perform in a particular way, if the signal isn't recognizable, somebody might conclude that the person doesn't know *how.* Another subtle obstacle to performance.

A Final Check on Assumptions

By now you've seen that the cause of a problem is not always what someone says it is. Assumptions may be made about the origin of a performance discrepancy, and it can sometimes take a lot of probing to learn what's truly happening. Take a look at these examples.

The Case of the Sleepy Workers

The training director of a dynamite factory overseas told of an instance where all the training in the world would have been useless in solving the problem.

He was called by a plant manager. "I've got a training problem," said the manager. "These people are lazy. Many fall asleep on the job, and they don't come to work regularly. I want you to come up here and teach them their jobs. I want you to teach them to be motivated."

The training director was too smart to fall into the trap of taking a statement like that at face value, especially since it began with the usual confusion of problem with solution. Knowing his human relations, he replied, "I'll come and take a look around so that I can see more clearly what needs to be taught." (It doesn't get you very far to tell a client that his or her diagnosis is probably wrong. It works better to agree that there is a problem and then do your analysis out loud, hoping that *the client* will spot the difficulty.)

The training director went to the site, looked around, talked to people, and reviewed employee records. All the while, he was asking himself whether he was dealing with a skill deficiency—and, if not, why the men were not performing as expected.

He found the answer in an unexpected place—the medical office. Better than 60 percent of the employees in question were suffering from a disease that shows up in symptoms of sleeping sickness. *Of course* these men were falling asleep on the job. *Of course* their attendance was spotty.

But there wasn't anything wrong with their skill or with their motivation. They were simply sick. Once cured, all was well. Until those medical records were checked, though, no one even guessed that the obstacle to performing as desired was physiological.

Again, all the training in the world would not have done much good. Had the training director simply done what he was asked, his training program would have failed. Then the plant manager might have said, "Why spend all this money on a training department? We'd be better off without 'em." And what's more, if the training department continually used training as a solution for the wrong problems, he'd be right.

———

Thus, if performance discrepancies appear *not* to be due to a lack of skill or motivation, one thing to look for is the *obstacle*. "I can't do it" isn't always just an alibi; it can be an accurate description of the situation. And if you will look around to see what might be obstructing performance, you will find the solution to at least some of your performance problems.

———

The Case of the Parisian Training Problem

Not all performance problems arise so neatly from a single, major cause, underlining the caution not to leap in and proclaim, "Aha! That's the problem!"

Imagine yourself being called in by the personnel director of a French department store and being asked to solve a training problem. Specifically, you are asked to develop a sales course for clerks. At this point you have no information about *why* the course is needed (you don't know whether there are performance discrepancies, and if so, how large they may be), and so you don't yet know whether instruction is needed. Clearly, more information is needed.

On questioning, the director reveals that he wants sales training because "gross receipts are not what they should be."

Now the amount of money taken in by a store is only partly related to the skill of its salesclerks. Since further questioning fails to elicit information directly related to salesclerks and their abilities, you begin to wonder if the cause of the problem might be elsewhere. You ask to be shown around the store. Within a few minutes, you note several clumps of people gathered around cash registers, trying to give the clerks money to complete transactions. Why was it so difficult to buy something? The amount of paperwork the clerks had to put up with was daunting.

Next, you find that some merchandise was placed on the counters according to manufacturer rather than according to type. Someone wanting to look at transistor radios, for example, might first have to go to the Phillips department (on the main floor) to see what they had and then walk to the Telefunken department (one floor up at the other end of the store) to see what merchandise was available there. (And there were more than twelve departments in the store that sold some form of rubber hose.)

In some ways, this is typical of the situations wrongly labeled "training problems." Basically, what is wrong is that management has rushed to a solution without first looking at other elements of the problem. Here, as in most situations involving those infinitely variable entities called people, there is probably no perfect solution to yield a perfect answer. But there are usually some solutions that are superior to others in terms of return for effort expended.

It's not too much to say that the management of this store singled out the element that was most visible (the salesclerks) and most under its control and made it the scapegoat for an important discrepancy. They then identified a solution that involved changing the salesclerks in some way.

The trouble with premature identification of solutions is that it blocks off exploration of other problem elements. We tend to say to ourselves, "Well, that's that. We've nailed down what we're going to do. Now let's get on with doing it." Because we feel, "We're doing something about it," some of the burden of the problem has been lifted from our shoulders.

It's probably clear, however, that other elements contributed to the store's problem. In studying the procedures, it became plain that the store's merchandising policies almost seemed designed to prevent customers from buying; or, having once bought, to discourage them from coming back again. It was hard to find what one wanted; it was hard to complete a purchase. Once the merchandising procedures were revised and the time to complete a transaction was reduced, sales increased.

The Case of the Frustrated Shopper

Sometimes the obstacle blocking performance is not caused by entangling procedures; rather, desired performance is hampered by a shortage of resources. Let's say that your "job" is to go to the store to buy something. When you get there you find that there isn't anyone to answer questions or help you find what you're looking for. Doesn't this make your shopping "job" harder than need be? Will the frustration cause you to avoid this store next time around? Aren't stores like this shooting themselves in their collective feet with a performance discrepancy based on a misguided attempt at economy?

The world of retail selling has given us many other examples. For instance, way back when, in the days when the first retail computer stores opened, the sales staffs consisted largely of computer programmers. Someone had decided that programmers were the only ones who knew enough about the products to sell them. The result, though, was largely exasperating to the customer. Customers could stand there waving a fistful of money until closing time and never be noticed, because the "sales" staff was busy playing at the terminals. The customers knew how to give clerks money, so there was no skill deficiency involved. They wanted to buy the products, so there wasn't a motivation issue. What there was, though, was a large obstacle preventing the customers from performing (buying) the way they wanted to perform.

Update: If you can't speak the buzzwords of computing—which seem to change every week—have you tried to get advice from someone working in a present-day computer store? (The more things change, the more they stay the same.)

The Case of the Timid Golfer

One of our colleagues tells this story:

"I'd always wanted to play golf, so I took a golf course in college. They taught me how to hold a club, how to swing, and I was all set. And yet, after the course ended, it was seven years before I actually played on a public course."

"What stopped you?" we asked.

"They didn't teach me how to *get onto* a golf course, and I was embarrassed at the thought of not knowing the ropes."

It may seem like a small impediment to you, but it kept our friend from enjoying the sport he's enjoyed ever since.

The Case of the Diffident Dancer

PP: Bob, didn't you have a similar experience with your dancing lessons?

RFM: Yes. When I decided to take tap lessons when I turned 55, it was six weeks before I could screw up the courage to call a dance studio.

PP: What prevented you?

RFM: It wasn't skill—I knew how to look up a number and use the phone. It was the thought of this gray-haired man clomping around amongst a bevy of leotard-clad little girls that stopped me. When I did finally look in the phone book, it was another six weeks before I selected a number to call.

PP: And when you finally gathered the courage to call?

RFM: Once I called it was smooth sailing. But not knowing what to expect was a real obstacle, and the way the ads were written just made it worse.

It's no good to just sit there thinking, "That was no obstacle, that was just stupidity. All he had to do was call and get the information he needed." Remember Cram's law:* People don't do things for the damnedest reasons.

Those last two examples are both about obstacles caused by reluctance to step through a door to new experiences (unjustified, as it turns out, since both came out with happy endings) of looking foolish in an unfamiliar situation. If lack of information keeps people from approaching situations in which they would like to be involved, it doesn't help to charge them with "stupidity" or to write off their doubts to "poor motivation." Since we're in the business of getting rid of obstacles to performance once they've been identified, our task is to address the obstacle and try to close the gap between what we've got and what we need. Most of us will not always "boldly go" into new experiences. Just as the golfer needed a lesson on "how to get on the golf course," there's a need in other situations for a similar transition easing the anguish of that first step into uncharted territory. It's always wise, therefore, to wonder if there isn't something subtle preventing the performer from getting started on the tasks at hand.

---

* Periodically muttered by Dr. David Cram, who also *does* things for the damnedest reasons.

―――――――――

The Case of Sagging Production

These impediments to performance can take many forms and may appear in unlikely places. A few years ago, one of us was asked to review a division of a company and make whatever recommendations for improvement seemed appropriate. Things were going pretty well, so this was not one of the instances that begins with "I've got a training problem." Production was down a little, but it was not a matter of panic proportions, although puzzling.

As is customary, two or three days were spent soaking in the activities of the division, working from inspectors of incoming material toward the loading dock.

It was learned that though production was sagging, nothing else had changed. There was no new product that people had to learn how to build. The same employees were still on the scene. There were no new, complicated machines to master. There seemed to be no morale or personality problems of any significance. Parts were flowing smoothly to the supply bins located at one end of the production floor. Tools were plentiful and in good working order.

Then what? The answer, the ridiculous answer, was discovered while sitting with some spot welders at their workbenches. It was noticed that they were rather slow in getting up to refill the empty parts bins on their benches. Why? They were one stool short on the production floor! Getting up meant that a welder's stool might be gone when she returned. So each woman dawdled when her bins were empty, and each spent time carving her initials or taping identifying marks on "her" stool.

For want of a stool . . . Clearly this was an obstacle to desired performance, but one not easily spotted with the naked eye.

―――――――――

Summing Up

In summary, before settling on solutions, look for subtle impediments to performance. Look for things that might be getting in the way of their performing as desired. Look for:

- Lack of authority, lack of time, or lack of tools.
- Poorly placed or poorly labeled equipment.
- Bad lighting and uncomfortable surroundings.
- Lack of *direct* information about *what* to do and *when* to do it.
- Competition from secondary tasks within the job itself and from the actions (or inactions) of other people.
- The "nobody told me" problem. There's usually no excuse for secret agendas or conflicting policies.

Above all, keep in mind that if they can do it but aren't doing it, there is a reason; only seldom is the reason either a lack of interest or a lack of desire. Most people want to do a good job. When they don't, it is often because of an obstacle in the world around them.

Be aware that the assumed cause and effect are not always accurate and that the true origins of problems are not always obvious. Problems often surface downstream from the place where they originate.

Any time it seems that there's no cause for a discrepancy— that is, it doesn't seem due to a lack of skill or motivation— keep looking; you still haven't found the obstacle. Widen your search.

Finally: First you state the problem *and the cause,* then you devise solutions. Having a "solution in search of a problem" is not a recommended approach.

What to Do

Determine whether there are subtle obstacles preventing expected performance.

How to Do It

Ask these questions:

- What prevents this person from performing?

- Does the person know what is expected?

- Does the person know when to do what is expected?

- Are there conflicting demands on this person's time?

- Is there competition from secondary tasks?

- Are there restrictive policies that ought to be changed?

- Can I reduce "competition from the job"—phone calls, "brush fires," demands of less important but more immediate problems?

- Could the problem be caused upstream from where the consequences are being felt?

12
Do They Have What It Takes?

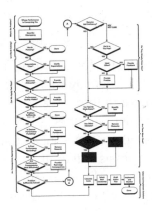

WHERE WE ARE

An important performance discrepancy has been identified, and it has been discovered that it is a genuine skill deficiency. Before moving on, however, we need to know whether the performers in question are "right" for the job.

By this point in the analysis, you may have several ideas about how to tackle the different causes of genuine deficiencies in performance. Keep them on "hold" until you have explored another issue by asking: Do the non-performers have the potential to benefit from this change? In plain language, do they have what it takes to learn what they don't now know?

You can make all the changes you like; but if an individual doesn't have what it takes, either mentally or physically, to do the job, the changes are a waste of time.

Any time someone cannot handle an existing job, you're stuck, inevitably, with the two universal alternatives to all of the solutions proposed in this book: Change the job or change the person. The first alternative was discussed in previous chapters. The second is the subject of this chapter.

"Changing the person" means, of course, to substitute another individual (or a machine) for the apparent non-performer. Sometimes it's quite plain that this is inevitable, as when physical limitations prevent performance. The decision to transfer or fire, however, is not always as straightforward as it may seem when your patience is running out. In fact, to look at a problem with anger or impatience is to look at it through a distorting lens.

The Case of Getting an Eyeful

On a production line making very tiny products, for example, a foreman complained that one woman made considerably more mistakes than anyone else. Like the others, she peered through a binocular microscope to see the tiny parts and to assist with their assembly. She assembled the same product as the others, and under the same conditions. But she was considerably "clumsier" than the others. The foreman wanted to get rid of her—that was his solution.

This case came to the attention of the department concerned with training and performance, and its members looked around and asked questions. They quickly discovered that this worker was not looking through the microscope with both eyes as she should have been. She looked with only one eye at a time. She didn't know that looking with both eyes at the same time made any difference when the instrument was properly adjusted. But without the depth perception that comes with using both eyes simultaneously, she could not see well enough to assemble accurately. Hence, she was labeled "clumsy."

After only two or three *minutes* of instruction in the proper use of the microscope, the woman's work was the equal of all the others in the department. She wasn't clumsy, or unmotivated, or incapable of learning. She was simply prevented from doing the job well by lack of information. In this example, "transfer or terminate" was not the remedy—a little bit of training was.

The remedies of transfer and termination are used more often than they should be. They are the crude hatchets of those unsophisticated in their knowledge of the limits of human performance, a sign of failure to locate less traumatic remedies. They should be considered a last resort rather than a first.

The issue of "potential to perform" should be approached in two stages: Could the person learn the job? Does he or she have what it takes to do the job?

If people can learn a job, they can do it, can't they? Not necessarily. It sounds contradictory, but some people become under-performers because they are overqualified for the job.

Some companies court trouble without realizing it by following a policy of over-hiring. "We always hire the best people available," they boast; then they go on to set people to work at jobs that are beneath their abilities. College graduates are put to work as glorified typists or given simple tasks on a production line; engineers find themselves working in the drafting department. Managers who succumb to this temptation are bewildered when dissatisfaction appears in its many guises—low morale, absenteeism, edginess, uncooperativeness, and so on.

The Case of the Expensive Interpreter

In a company we know, inspectors tested some complex electronic devices at the end of assembly. They did so by connecting the devices to their test equipment and checking readings on dials. The day-shift inspector was an older woman who had little idea of why she was doing these things. She did what she was trained to do and hooked up the devices and recorded the readings. If the readings deviated from those specified, she rejected the device.

The night-shift inspection, on the other hand, was handled by a young woman who was a doctoral candidate in the arts at a nearby university. She found an intellectual challenge in any task. To counteract her boredom with the job routine, she worked hard at finding out all she could about the how and why of the manufacture of the devices. Eventually, she was able to hold an intelligent conversation about the devices with engineers. Because of her increased knowledge, she began to *interpret* the readings on her test equipment. She no longer adhered to the strict accept/reject instructions of her training. As a result, she began to accept devices that should *not* have been accepted and to send others back for expensive reworking when they *should* have been accepted.

It's always a temptation to put the "best" available person into a job. But when that person is much overqualified, the rewards can be short-lived. A more realistic matching of skills with jobs will avoid the boredom and lack of challenge that lead to performance discrepancies after the first rush of enthusiasm.

The Case of the Reluctant Garbage Carrier

The problem of over-qualification can arise at home, too. Take the case of the teenager assigned to the carrying-out-the-garbage detail. The young are notoriously (and perhaps rightly) impatient of activities they consider boring. So the teenager fights carrying out the garbage.

"I'm his father/mother," you say. "Why should I get stuck with this chore when I have this son/daughter sitting around? Isn't it boring for me, too?" Yes, of course. But emotional issues aside, the teenager is bored and wants to be involved in something more exciting. Garbage-carrying loses out when it competes with doing, or even dreaming about, most other activities. The rewards of garbage-carrying have to be competitive with those real or imagined delights—a good trick. The least this tells you is that those who work at tasks for which they are overqualified need some extrinsic reward to take the place of "satisfaction in the job."

Following the lead discussed in the previous chapter, you may wonder whether the task can be simplified or made more interesting. Why is there so much garbage? Could the amount be reduced? (Eat your spinach!) If it could, that might make for fewer trips to the can. How about installing a disposal or a trash masher? That might reduce the number of trips still further.

How about making the task more interesting? One father we know claims he hasn't had any trouble at all getting the kids to mow the lawn—since he bought a motorized lawn mower that they can sit on and drive!

Are They Right for the Job?

Meanwhile, back to the point of this chapter. "Do they have the potential?" refers only in part to intellectual capacity, as mentioned earlier. *Appropriateness* for the task or job is another facet to consider. A person may have all the mental and physical qualities needed to do the job and still be wrong for it.

"I suppose I could learn to fill out that evil tax form, but I'll hate it."

"Sure I can do the job, but I just don't like to work in cold weather. You just might as well not send me there in the first place."

"I can do the job OK, but I just hate doing it with that music blaring all day long."

"No, I don't *want* to do that job, no matter how good I might get at it."

"I love photography, but I'm a little too claustrophobic to work in a darkroom."

In each case the person is wrong for the job, whatever it may be. There's a lack of inclination. When people so plainly announce themselves to be square pegs, they lack the potential for sustained performance.

Summing Up

In summary, it is useful to determine whether someone has the capacity to do the job required, and whether he or she would "fit" the job mentally and motivationally, even if the performance in question were brought up to standard. If the answer to both questions is "yes," go ahead with your analysis. If not, replace the performer with someone more suited to the job.

What to Do

Determine whether the person has the potential to perform as desired.

How to Do It

Ask these questions:

- Could the person learn the job (is the individual trainable)?

- Does this person have the physical and mental potential to perform as desired?

- Is this person over-qualified for the job?

- Is this person right for the job?

Part V

Which Solutions Are Best?

What should I do now?

Now that you've collected all the clues and potential solutions, it's time to decide which solution mix will come closest to solving the problem.

To do that, you'll need to think seriously about the cost of the problem, and about the cost of each of the best solutions, before making the final solution decision and drafting your action plan. This section will help you to do that.

13
Which Solution Is Best?

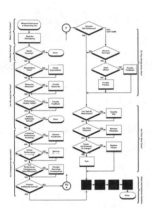

WHERE WE ARE

One or more solutions or remedies for a performance discrepancy have been identified. We need to find out what each solution would cost, so that we can select the most cost-effective combination.

Isn't this the end of the line? By now you probably have what looks like one or more relevant solutions, so why not put them to work? Because there's one more question to ponder before racing for the finish line: Will the results be worth the trouble? This can be a tougher question than it seems, and all too often it doesn't get the attention it deserves.

If you have followed the procedure we've described, you'll have concentrated on finding potential solutions for your problem, without too much regard for whether the solution is the most practical or feasible in your situation. As a result, one or more of the remedies you have generated may be inappropriate simply because they are beyond the resources you can bring to bear. Perhaps it's plain that you would not be able to get the money, perhaps it violates policy, or maybe you don't have the organizational "muscle" to implement it. Here's how to proceed.

1. Check the Feasibility of Each Solution.

As the first step in deciding which solution is best, ask these questions of each one:

- Is this possible solution clearly inappropriate or impossible to implement?
- Is this possible solution plainly beyond our resources?

When the answer to either of the questions is "Yes," put the solution aside for the moment. Don't discard these possibilities, though; someone may be able to show you how to put that "unworkable" solution into practice. Too many "It can't be done" and "It's against company policy" assertions have been shown to be untrue, so avoid being hasty about scrapping solutions that look impossible at first glance.

2. Determine the "Cost" of Each Solution.

The next step is to determine the "cost" of each remaining solution. Just as you affixed a value to each of the consequences of the discrepancy, now determine what it would cost to adopt each of the tentative solutions you developed during the analysis.

Why bother with each one? For two important reasons:

a. All too often, perhaps without realizing it, people lock onto a solution without giving "equal time" to other potential answers. The selected solution may be one they had even before doing the analysis; or it may be one that, on the face of it, is more "obviously" right than others. That's not to say that either of these types of solutions will never be the right one. But plunging too quickly for an answer without considering the cost of all alternatives deprives you of another advantage—the other important reason.

b. As you ponder costs, you will probably find yourself generating even more solutions, compromises, and combinations that are often more innovative and more appropriate than the original answers.

Solutions Aren't "Free"

Don't jump too quickly, either, to the conclusion that any solution comes free of cost. Consider, for example, the common problem of instructors who insult or humiliate their students in one way or another (such as forcing them to participate in ill-conceived role-plays). Someone notices and says:

"There's a discrepancy between what these instructors are doing and what they should be doing. We've got to do something about that."

"Fine. How will you get them to stop doing it?"

"Why, we'll tell them to stop."

So "telling" is proposed as the solution. And, on the face of it, this solution doesn't cost anything at all. All you have to do is to tell. But it isn't as simple as that, is it? Even if telling worked—which it seldom does—someone has to decide how the telling should happen. Will someone prepare a memo for all instructors? Will someone sit down with them in a group and tell? Or meet with them individually and tell? It is clear that when you think about the proposed solution in terms of "cost," it isn't as free as it looks. It may be quick and easy to do; but even for a solution of such dubious effectiveness, there is likely to be a "cost" in terms of someone's time, at the very least.

It's that way with most solutions. It "costs" somebody something to "do something." Perhaps not much, but something. When considering solutions, then, it is useful to estimate the cost of each tentative action. It will help prevent you from rushing off to implement a solution settled on before the analysis; it will help you to put the "obvious" solution into perspective; and it will help prevent you from implementing solutions that are more massive than the problem. After all, you wouldn't want to find yourself in the position of implementing hundred-thousand-dollar solutions to ten-thousand-dollar problems, or requiring ten people to involve themselves in a solution when a checklist would do as well.

Doing Nothing Can Be Expensive

Clearly, money is an important measuring instrument in decisions regarding solutions for performance discrepancies. After all, if you can't afford a particular solution, or if a solution costs more than the results are likely to be worth, plainly there is further analysis to be done. A less obvious case, perhaps, is that of doing nothing. The cost of the solution should be weighed against the cost of maintaining the status quo. What looks at first like an "unreasonable" cost may look considerably more attractive if the true cost of the present situation is examined. You proved this when you calculated the cost of the discrepancy back in Chapter 2. Calculating the size or "cost" of a discrepancy is the same as calculating the cost of doing nothing.

There's a tendency to say that an existing state of affairs "costs nothing" and that any solution that entails an added outlay of money therefore has to be more expensive. But the "hidden cost" of "doing nothing" about a performance discrepancy can be considerable—in inefficient performance, overly long or unnecessary courses, scrap piles larger than they need be, lost or angry customers, employee turnover and absenteeism, and varying degrees of frustration.

Intangible Costs

The paragraphs above may make it sound as though we are talking only about money when estimating solution costs. Not so. There are cost dimensions other than monetary ones, as a proposed solution will often require time, talent, people-dedication, hard work, and so on. These intangibles must not be ignored; and when included in the sum total of the solution requirement, the solution may not be worth the expected results.

Consider for a moment the "problem" of getting people to buckle their seat belts when driving. "People really oughta wanna wear their seat belts," goes the cry. What happens if they *don't?* Statistics are trotted out to "prove" that a certain number of people will die. And how much is a life worth? How much should we be willing to spend to prevent people from dying as a result of their own folly? Clearly, there are intangible costs incurred by letting the problem alone, and some intangible costs incurred by "solving" the problem (costs such as the loss of freedom to act as one wishes and belt-burn on the necks of shorter drivers, to mention only two).

In the United States, millions of dollars have been spent on bells, buzzers, interlocks, and widespread exhortation to "buckle up." This expensive "solution" hasn't worked very well. Elsewhere, better results have been achieved almost at the stroke of a pen. Australia, for example, has passed a law requiring a fine whenever, and for whatever reason, anyone is caught driving without a fastened seat belt. The result is better than 85 percent compliance, a far more successful solution than that of "throwing money at the problem."

But how to evaluate intangible costs? Most of the time it is easier than it looks. The procedure for evaluating intangible solution costs is threefold:

1. Name the intangibles;

2. Describe the components of people and effort that would be required to implement the solution; and

3. Describe the implications of implementation, whether they be political or personal.

The use of this procedure may not provide you with precise numbers, but it will put you in a better position to rank solutions in terms of total cost.

By the time you have identified an area of intangible costs and have described the amount of effort that will be involved, the practicality of the solution may be obvious. For example, once you see that cleaning up the neighborhood will take the efforts of 50 volunteers, and that it would take more organizing and bell-ringing and telephoning hours than you have to offer, the solution of "get the neighbors to do it" looks pretty unlikely, even without thinking about monetary aspects of the cost.

The Case of the Thieving Loan Officers

Intangible costs can come from any direction. Consider the plight of the training director of a large bank:

"We lose about a half-million dollars a year through bank robberies!"

"Sounds like a lot. What do you do about it?"

"Plenty. We hire more guards, we buy cameras and miles of videotape, we teach people complex defensive routines, and we buy other special equipment."

"How much does that cost?"

"Don't ask."

"You mean it costs more than half a million a year?"

"It sure does."

"Why do it if it costs more than the problem?"

"Well, it has value other than just deterring robberies. Our customers are reassured by knowing we have all the latest gadgets, and we look 'up-to-date' in the eyes of our peers. We feel that those results, unmeasurable though they may be, make it important to spend more on a solution than the problem is costing."

"Sounds like a wise decision."

"Well, it is and it isn't."

"Oh?"

"Well, we lose half a million a year in robberies, but we lose twenty-four million a year in loan losses."

"Wow! What do you do about that?"

"Nothing."

"Nothing?"

"Nothing. Most of that loss is caused by vice-presidents who fail to follow established loan procedure. They make loans against the better judgment established by policy, the loan goes sour, and we lose a bundle."

"Why isn't something done about the problem?"

"Ahh, it's called clout. The board or the president could do something about it, but my department doesn't have the clout. So we concentrate our efforts on preventing robberies."

Here was an instance in which a solution (preventing robberies) cost a lot more than the problem itself (the robberies), and in which a much bigger problem (the loan losses) was ignored. Isn't there an old saw having to do with goring oxen? (By the way, if you think we invented this episode, you're wrong.)

You can probably think of several instances in which the intangible (unmeasurable) costs of the solutions played a large part in the decision on just *which* solution would be tried. Once the intangible costs have been evaluated, the monetary aspect often pales in comparison.

3. Evaluate Solutions.

Which solution (or combination of solutions) is best? What action should you take? By now it's possible that one solution will stand out clearly as being better than the others you considered. The value of implementing the solution will clearly be positive. The solution will be:

- *economical* (considerably cheaper than the problem);
- *practical,* in that the means for implementing it are available to you; and
- *feasible,* in that it will be acceptable to the people affected and not harmful (politically or otherwise) to you or others.

Divide and Conquer

But what happens if all of your potential solutions are rejected because they were plainly beyond your resources? Or because, on close examination, they proved unfeasible or impractical?

The answer is the same for both. You will have to re-examine the problem and the solution to see if one or both can be scaled down. Ask:

- Can the problem be attacked in parts?
- Can a portion of the solution be used to solve a portion of the problem?

Sometimes it makes good sense to settle for less than the ultimate solution. If you shoot for something less than perfection, you may be able to get acceptable results for a good deal less effort. Or, when problems and solutions seem out of reach, it often makes sense to ask: What will give us the most result for the least effort? Which aspect are we best equipped to tackle? Which part of the problem interests us most? Which part of the problem is the most "visible" to those who must be pleased? So . . .

- If you can't afford to train 50 people, can you train five and have them provide on-the-job training for their colleagues?
- If you can't afford to hire all the guards indicated for plant security, can you shore things up sufficiently with closed-circuit TV?
- If you don't have room in the house for a piano, could your child learn to play the piccolo? Or an electronic keyboard?
- If you don't have the room or the teachers in your school to provide vital vocational training, can you persuade local industry to provide some space and know-how?
- If you can't provide the service to all, can you find a quick way to tell who needs the service most?
- If you can't find a foolproof way of telling whether ammunition is in working order other than by firing it, can you use a random-sampling technique that will be almost as good?

4. Draft an Action Plan.

A good way to test the feasibility of your solutions is to draft a simple action plan. For each possible solution, this plan briefly describes the answers to these two questions:

a. Who will be expected to implement this solution?

b. How will you get that person or persons to do what it will take to make the implementation happen?

It isn't enough simply to expect someone else to "change the policy," or "provide training," or "arrange feedback," or "get a law passed." Unless you say *who* will do it and *how* you will get that person to do it, your solutions may never be put into practice. Without an action plan, you might not cause yourself to think about what happens next. In addition, you would deprive yourself of an opportunity to test the cost of each solution. Here's an example.

Suppose you've analyzed a discrepancy having to do with engineers who seem totally uninterested in completing their paperwork by the allotted deadlines. During the analysis you discover that there are no significant consequences *to the engineers* whether or not they meet these deadlines. Obviously, one solution will be to arrange consequences, and arrange them in such a way that meeting deadlines leads to a favorable consequence *to the engineers,* and not meeting the deadlines leads to consequences that are considered unfavorable *by the engineers.*

How will you make that come to pass? Will you storm into the office of the manager and demand that consequences be arranged? Will you draft a description of some of the possible consequences that might be useful, and then send a memo to the engineers' manager outlining the cost of the problem, as well as your suggestions for a solution? Will you present the substance of your memo in person? What do *you* need to do to get this particular solution implemented? Your answer to this question will form a piece of your action plan. You would repeat the process for each of the solutions you intend to recommend.

Summing Up

In summary, answer the "What do I do now?" question by doing the following:

a. Collect all the potential solutions that address the issues revealed by your analysis (such as the need to reduce punishment of desired performance or the need to eliminate obstacles);

b. Determine or estimate the cost of implementing each solution;

c. Select the solution(s) that will add the most value (solve the largest part of the problem for the least effort); and then

d. Draft a brief action plan that describes, for each solution, how it will be put into practice and who will do the work.

What to Do

Estimate the cost of each potential solution, select the solution or combination of solutions that is most practical, feasible, and economical, and draft an action plan that describes who will implement each solution and how each solution will be implemented.

How to Do It

Answer these questions:

• Have all the potential solutions been identified?

• Does each solution address itself to one or more problems identified during the analysis (such as skill deficiency, absence of potential, incorrect rewards, punishing consequences, distracting obstacles)?

- Have all the problems identified been addressed?

- What is the cost of each potential solution?

- Have the intangible (unmeasurable) costs been assessed?

- Which solution (or combination of solutions) is most practical, feasible, and economical?

- Which solution will add most value (solve the largest part of the problem for the least effort)?

- Which solution are we best equipped to try?

- Which remedy interests us most? (Or, on the other side of the coin, which remedy is most visible to those who must be pleased?)

- Have I drafted an action plan that describes how each solution will be implemented and who will do the implementing?

Part VI

Quick-Reference
Checklist &
Final Thoughts

Now that the steps of our performance analysis procedure are familiar to you, we can summarize them for you in a Quick-Reference Checklist. Use the checklist as a guide, or as a way to help others see why they really oughta wanna re-evaluate solutions they have already decided upon.

We also offer a few final suggestions for applying the performance analysis procedure in the world around you.

A
Quick-Reference
Checklist

I. Describe the Problem

1. What is the performance discrepancy?

- Whose performance is at issue?
- Why is there said to be a problem?
- What is the actual performance at issue?
- What is the desired performance?

2. Is it worth pursuing?

- What would happen if I let it alone?
- Are our expectations reasonable?
- What are the consequences caused by the discrepancy?
- Is that cost enough to justify going on?

II. Explore Fast Fixes

3. Can we apply fast fixes?

- Do those concerned know what is expected of them?
- Can those concerned describe desired performance? Expected accomplishments?
- Are there obvious obstacles to performance?
- Do these people get feedback on how they are doing?

III. Check Consequences

4. Is desired performance punishing?

- What are the consequences of performing as desired?
- Is it actually punishing or perceived as punishing?

5. Is undesired performance rewarding?

- What rewards, prestige, status, or comfort support the present way of doing things?
- Does misbehaving get more attention than doing it right?

6. Are there any consequences at all?

- Does desired performance lead to consequences that the performer sees as favorable?

IV. Enhance Competence

7. Is it a skill deficiency?

- Could they do it if their lives depended on it, i.e., could they do it if they really had to?

8. Could they do it in the past?

- Could they once perform the task but have forgotten how?

9. Is the skill used often?

- How often is the performance displayed?
- How often is the skill applied?
- Is there feedback on how things are going? Is the feedback available regularly?

10. **Can the task be simplified?**

- Particularly for "hurry up" demands, can I reduce the standards by which performance is judged?
- Can I provide some sort of performance aid?
- Can I redesign the workplace or provide other physical help?
- Can I parcel off part of the job to someone else or arrange a job swap?

11. **Any obstacles remaining?**

- Does something get in the way of doing it right?
- Lack of knowledge about what's expected?
- Conflicting demands?
- Restrictive policies?

12. **Do they have what it takes?**

- Is it likely that this person could learn to do the job?
- Does this person lack the physical or mental potential to perform as desired?
- Is this person over-qualified for this job?

V. Develop Solutions

13. **Which solution is best?**

- Have all potential solutions been identified?
- Does each address one or more parts of the problem(s)?
- Have estimates of any intangible costs of the problem(s) been included?
- What is the cost of each potential solution?
- Which solution(s) are most practical, feasible, and economical?
- Which yields most value, solving the largest part of the problem(s) for least effort?

B
In the Real World

In this book we've described a way to analyze a particular kind of problem—those involving discrepancies between desired and actual human performance. Though it may seem to have taken a long time to describe, it doesn't take nearly as long to *do*. After a little practice, you will find yourself quickly ticking your mental way through the key questions, sometimes taking only a few seconds to see a problem in a new light—and to identify a likely solution. You will find, too, that after you've practiced the analysis a few times, you won't be able to keep from looking at the world through your performance analysis lenses.

To survive, however, you'll have to remind yourself that people usually don't do apparently dumb things on purpose, that they actually believe their way of doing things is pretty good. That's one reason you'll run across many situations which, for one reason or other, are so obviously out of whack that you'll wonder how anything ever gets done.

For example, you'll hear executives say they want their products to be user-friendly, yet they won't seek input from human-factors specialists until the product has been manufactured. You'll hear them talk about the need for boosting productivity, all the while soaking up thousands of employee hours with purposeless meetings. You'll find CEOs pitting one division against another in a race for results, only to wonder why, as a consequence, there is no communication among them. You'll run across managers who squeeze out their most experienced employees (often referred to as early retirement), then wonder why new-hires aren't as competent as the people just discarded. (For a crystal-clear picture of how the world actually works, there's a book that contains all the wisdom of the ages. It's called *The Dilbert Principle,* by Scott Adams.)

You'll notice schools that give diplomas to people who can't read, write, or make change, causing industry to spend millions to right this wrong. And you'll notice that the consequences are felt by industry and by the graduates, not by those causing the problem; no consequences, in other words, to those turning out the non-functional adults.

But there's a brighter world at the end of the tunnel, because there is growing realization that people act as they do for reasons other than malicious intent. Those in charge are learning that it's possible to attack performance problems by methods other than by finger-pointing, exhortation, and threats. They're learning that training isn't always the magic solution when unsatisfactory performance is detected. And they're learning that it's OK to ask for help.

As time goes by, therefore, you'll be more and more likely to be asked to help with problems of human performance. Typically, you'll be asked to solve one performance problem—the one the client recognizes—that probably lives in a sea of others. Navigating these waters successfully requires somewhat more than performance analysis skill. So in closing, we'd like to offer some thoughts to help you on your road to blazing success.

Handholds Along The Walk Of Life

- Control your face and words. Performance analysis skill will allow you to see disjoints and mismanagement in the world around you. When working with clients you will be well served to control your snickers and your words when your understanding of the situation allows you to see solutions invisible to the client.

- Expect and look for hidden agendas; they're everywhere. Rarely will people begin by telling you either the true problem or the real reason they want it solved. As you've learned, most people can't distinguish between problems and solutions (e.g., "I've got a training problem."). So keep asking questions, keep on observing, until you're confident that you've learned how things are and why they are as they are.

- Respect the client. There are reasons why things are being done the way they are. They may not be good reasons—or even rational reasons. Nonetheless, your clients may have a great deal of themselves invested in the *status quo;* they may not take kindly to an implication that their way isn't the best way or to the thought that for years they've been doing it wrong. Remember, too, that when you propose a solution to a problem, you're also proposing that someone needs to do something differently—to *change.* And willingness to change may not increase in proportion to the size or seriousness of the problem.

  Before proposing your solutions, therefore, ask yourself how you would feel if someone proposed to you what you are about to propose to them. And ask yourself whether your proposed changes are realistic in light of what you know about the situation. Tell yourself that you're in the business of making things better than they were, and the struggle for perfection may not be realistic or feasible. Then treat them as you would be treated, i.e., do unto others . . .

- Respect client values. People aren't necessarily wrong because their values differ from your own, and their habits and practices don't necessarily have to be "fixed" because they don't match your own ideas of goodness and efficiency. When you enter your clients' territory, tell yourself that you're visiting someone's home. Though you may be there to solve a specific problem, you won't have been invited there to solve *all* the problems. So be a good guest. Think about the destitute plumber who, when asked to fix a leaky toilet, couldn't refrain from offering advice on how to improve the customers' child-rearing practices. Similar behavior can make you destitute, too.

- Allow your client to save face. For example, never blurt out the solution to a performance problem until you've walked through the analysis together. The client has lived with this problem for some time without seeing the solution(s). If, in your excitement, you verbalize these solutions too early, your client may feel belittled and insulted. Enjoy your ability to make sense out of things, but try not to offer solutions until you understand the environment in which the problem lives.

- Let your client solve the problem. Do your analysis "out loud," asking questions and reflecting answers; often, the client will suddenly make the connection between problem and solution. When that happens, you won't have to "sell" the solution or work as hard to get it implemented. (And there's nothing wrong with allowing a bit of social banter into your analysis discussions, relaxing the mood and allowing time for insights to spring forth.)

Epilogue

If you analyze *your* performance problems systematically, you may even come to view some of the larger problems of the world from a new vantage point and understand why some of the "tried and true" solutions are so ineffective. You may, for example, find new ways of thinking and responding to such comments as:

"Politicians oughta wanna reduce government spending."

"Posters hung in public places will help reduce the incidence of traffic deaths."

"People should take more responsibility for their own health."

"The government oughta wanna get off our backs."

"People oughta wanna make the government obey the Constitution."

"More people oughta wanna take responsibility for their own health."

Our checklist won't help you to understand *everything* about why people behave as they do. But if each of us could perceive more clearly the nature of just *one* important human problem—and throw his or her weight behind a solution related to the cause—we might just move bigger and more important things than mountains. It's worth a try.

We leave you with this final thought: Those who work to *solve* problems are more highly valued than those who merely label them.

Part VII
Appendices

C
Reprisal!

Every book should have a little corner from which authors are allowed to strike back. After all, several dozen individuals have had a go at our thoughts and at our manuscript—picking and probing, suggesting this, trampling on that, or just staring blankly at a mangled explanation they really should have understood.

Such knavery cannot go unsung—so sing we will. We wave the banner of acclaim for all those who so patiently allowed themselves to be battered by earlier, more primitive explanations of the concepts presented herein, and who were magnanimous enough to batter back.

More pointedly, we skewer with the lance of laud and commendation these generous souls who took pains to try on one or another of our later drafts and tell us just where it pinched and how the fit could be improved: John McCann, Rodney Cron, Randy Mager, Maryjane Rees, Vernon Rees, Andy Stevens, Walter Thorne, and Tom Watts.

And we hurry to lance (and laud, of course) those who so generously hacked and slashed their way through this new edition:

David Cram, Dan Raymond, Bonnie Abney, Ennis Pipe, Eileen Mager, and Paul Staples, as well as our favorite editress, Slash-'n-Burn Mary Kitzmiller.

Long may they dangle!

Robert F. Mager
Peter Pipe

D

For Further Reading

Gilbert, T. F. *Human Competence: Engineering Worthy Performance,* ISPI Tribute Edition. International Society for Performance Improvement, 1996.

Kerr, S. "On the Folly of Rewarding A, While Hoping for B," *Academy of Management Executive,* Volume IX, Number 1, February, 1995.

Zemke, R. *Figuring Things Out.* Reading, Mass.: Addison-Wesley Publishing Co., 1982.

Zigon, J. "Rewards and Performance Incentives," *Performance & Instruction,* International Society for Performance Improvement, Volume 33, number 10, 1994.

Index

Learn an easy to use process for finding realistic solutions to even the most difficult performance problems

The Solving Performance Problems Workshop

This workshop puts into action the principles found in Dr. Robert F. Mager and Peter Pipe's classic bestseller, *Analyzing Performance Problems*. This groundbreaking work led the way to the move from the focus on just training to today's broader focus on performance improvement.

In just one day, the *Solving Performance Problems Workshop* gives you the tools and know-how to wipe out performance problems that plague your company daily. You can save your organization untold dollars every year by eliminating those time-consuming people problems that cause managers to spend valuable time "putting out fires".

Who Should Attend

Managers, training professionals, training executives, human resource professionals and anyone else who solves performance issues.

You'll Learn a Valuable Process that Increases Your Own Credibility and Worth!

Conducted in a small group setting, you'll receive expert coaching and leave with the skills to:

- Zero in on what people *are doing* versus what they *should be* doing.
- Quickly figure out what the true cause of a problem is
- Know when training will help solve a problem—and when it won't
- Discover what problems *really* cost your organization.
- Assess which problems are even worth solving
- Recommend solutions that you know will work, including easy to do fast-fixes that have an immediate impact

You'll leave with your own personal toolkit you can continue to use long after the workshop ends, including the *Solving Performance Problems Software.*

Call 1-800-558-4237 for current dates and locations, or register online at www.cepworldwide.com.

Tuition
$375 per person

Bring this Workshop On-Site: If you have a group of people to train, it may make sense for us to come to you. Call us at 800-558-4237 for details and customization options.

MORE GREAT BOOKS FROM DR. ROBERT F. MAGER!

Dr. Robert F. Mager has authored one of the most extensive and renowned collections of books and resources on issues of human performance in existence today. These books are considered to be *the* reference library for anyone serious about educating others and improving human performance. You'll find everything you need to learn how to:

• develop successful instruction,
• find realistic solutions to performance problems,
• measure the results of your instruction,
• generate positive attitudes in learners,
• and much more!

Order your copies today and get resources you'll use for a lifetime.

	Quantity	x Price=	Total
Measuring Instructional Results *How to determine whether your instructional results have been achieved*		x $23.95=	
Preparing Instructional Objectives *A critical tool in the development of effective instruction*		x $22.95=	
How to Turn Learners On... without turning them off *Ways to ignite interest in learning*		x $22.95=	
Analyzing Performance Problems *How to figure out why people aren't doing what they should be, and what to do about it*		x $23.95=	
Making Instruction Work *A step-by-step guide to designing and developing instruction that works*		x $24.95=	
Goal Analysis *How to clarify your goals so you can actually achieve them*		x $22.95=	
The How to Write a Book Book		x $17.95=	
Life In The Pinball Machine		x $22.95=	
What Every Manager Should Know About Training		x $22.95=	
Subtotal			
Shipping & Handling*			
GA & TX residents add 7% sales tax to the subtotal plus shipping and handling			
Total Order			

* *Please add $6.00 for the first book, plus $1.50 for each additional book. Please allow four weeks for delivery by UPS Ground Service.*

Name _____

Phone _____ Fax _____

Organization _____

Address _____

City _____ State _____ Zip _____

☐ My check or money order for $_____ is enclosed

Charge my ☐ Visa ☐ Mastercard ☐ AmEx   Exp. Date _____

Card Number _____

Name on Card _____

Please send this form and your check, money order, or credit card number to:

CEP
P.O. Box 102462
Atlanta, GA 30368-2462

Call 1-800-558-4CEP for volume discount information.

Call for shipping charges on international orders.

For credit card orders, fax this order for faster delivery:
(770) 458-9109 or use our website at:
www.cepworldwide.com